MARIHUANA TODAY

A Compilation of
Medical Findings
for the Layman by
GEORGE K. RUSSELL

The Myrin Institute for Adult Education
521 Park Avenue, New York, N.Y. 10021

Marihuana Today is distributed in cooperation
with The American Council on Marijuana and
Other Psychoactive Drugs, Inc.

Marihuana Today

Revised edition 1978.

Marihuana Today was first published as Proceedings Number 29 of the Myrin Institute.

The Myrin Institute believes that a reconciliation of the modern scientific attitude with a spiritual world-concept is the most essential need of modern man.

Copyright © 1975, 1978 by The Myrin Institute, Inc. for Adult Education, 521 Park Avenue, New York, New York 10021.

ISBN 0-913098-27-2
Library of Congress Catalog Card No. 77-79477

Table of Contents

About the Author

Dr. George K. Russell is Professor of Biology at Adelphi University, Garden City, New York. A 1959 graduate of Princeton University, he was awarded a doctorate in biology by Harvard University in 1963, where he specialized in genetics, biochemistry and cellular physiology. Dr. Russell held postdoctoral fellowships from the National Science Foundation at Cornell University and Brandeis University. He taught biology at Princeton from 1965 to 1967 before joining the Adelphi faculty. At Adelphi, Dr. Russell teaches Freshman Biology, General Genetics and Molecular Biology. He is also currently engaged in research on the genetics, biochemistry and developmental physiology of *Euglena* and *Chlamydomonas* and has actively published in this field.

Preface to the Third Edition

The continuing growth of marihuana use and its increasing potency have prompted grave concern in the scientific community over mental and physical risks both to current users and future generations. Consequently, the past few years have witnessed considerable research by scientists around the world into the drug's effects on the body and mind, with the result that each year much new information is uncovered.

In July, 1978, approximately 50 papers on the subject were presented at the Second International Symposium on Marihuana in Reims, France.* Among the findings set forth at that time were Dr. Harris Rosenkrantz's precise and thorough studies concerning the deleterious effects of marihuana on the respiratory system and on embryological development, resulting from cannabis administration to laboratory animals in doses carefully established (by direct measurement of cannabis products in the blood) to correspond with levels of human consumption. Dr. Ethel Sassenrath presented equally important data on marihuana and embryonic development in primates, and Dr. Robert G. Heath added detailed findings with the electron microscope to his study of many years concerning marihuana's effects on the brain. Important, too, is the

*A monograph of the full proceedings of the VII International Congress of Pharmacology's Symposium on Marihuana will be published by Pergamon Press (New York and Oxford) in the spring of 1979 as *Marihuana and Membranes: Quantitation, Metabolism, Cellular Responses, Reproduction and Brain* (Nahas, G.G. and Paton, W.D.M. eds.).

development by Dr. Vincent Marks and his colleagues of a method for measuring cannabis products in human blood and urine, allowing, for instance, the proof of marihuana use before a fatal car accident.

Many thousands of young people, parents, educators and other professionals have read the earlier editions of *Marihuana Today*. Clearly from their responses, this "compilation of medical findings for the layman" has been one of the most helpful publications of its kind in informing the public about this subtle and insidious drug. The third edition, which includes highlights of the Reims Symposium as well as other new material, should be all the more important.

Those who have read the earlier editions may well note the developing trend of evidence: how cellular damage by cannabis, originally hotly debated, is increasingly authenticated; how tolerant and substantial abstinence effects are now established; how actions on the reproductive system and on development become increasingly worrying. In recent years there has been an asymmetry in the cannabis literature. On the one hand, strong pro-cannabis propaganda; on the other, many people of all ages (Dr. Russell cites a dean of students as one example), who see what they suspect to be adverse effects of marihuana smoking, yet remain silent for lack of knowledge of the documentary evidence. The time may well be coming, and this book will help greatly, when they discover that what they have seen themselves has, after all, scientific backing, and will feel freer to speak and act accordingly.

Some may question whether marihuana use is a matter of such importance in comparison to other problems confronting them. Yet it is special in this sense, that its damaging effects strike at brain and personality so that the capacity to make decisions about important matters is impaired. Dr. Russell's last words in the book put it so well, that although their force can be best appreciated after reading the book, I should like to quote them here:

> I wish therefore to leave one question with the reader: Can the use of marihuana, in *any* amount, ever be reconciled with the clarity of thought, the personal integrity and the strength of will that an individual must have who would play an active

role in helping humanity find the way out of its presently severe and ever-worsening difficulties?

W.D.M. Paton, C.B.E., F.R.C.P., F.R.S.
Professor of Pharmacology
University of Oxford
Fellow of Balliol College, Oxford
October, 1978

Preface to the Second Edition

The first edition of *Marihuana Today* was published in the spring of 1975 and had an immediate success. It is one of the most succinct yet scholarly statements available to the lay public on the physical and psychological effects of marihuana. After an initial distribution of 1,500 copies, the Myrin Institute, which had sponsored the article, was deluged by schools, churches, drug centers, civic organizations, certain branches of the armed forces and concerned parents with requests for copies.

Four printings later, because the demand was increasing rather than diminishing, the Institute had in mind to update *Marihuana Today* by including new data that had appeared since its original publication. Knowing of my enthusiasm for Dr. Russell's article and the fact that my wife and I had just completed a new book, *Sensual Drugs: Deprivation and Rehabilitation of the Mind,* * in which we reviewed in detail these most recent findings on marihuana, the editors asked if I would assist in the revision. I examined the pamphlet and found that very little editing would be needed. Indeed, the only changes I recommended were brief summaries of the latest data reported at the Helsinki conference on marihuana in 1975, new findings on the drug's effects on the brain, and the possible effects on the body of the estrogen-like properties of marihuana. While there could have been extensive reporting on this and other new material, I recognized the value of keeping *Marihuana Today* short.

It is my sincere hope that the scientific findings set forth in the following pages will be sufficient to discourage the spread and use of marihuana. In the end, however, all scientific evidence, necessary as it is for a full understanding of the drug's effects, may be meaningless unless the individual user sees what is happening to him or her as a result of the drug and sincerely desires to make a change. When I have challenged my own students at Berkeley—most of whom were convinced that marihuana did not affect their performance in any way—to abandon use of the drug for a period of three months and to make careful notes of any changes they noticed in their attitude or performance, they almost invariably came back to me at the end of this time and reported in approximately these words: "You know, Professor, I wouldn't have believed it possible, but you were right. I feel as though a layer of fog has been lifted from my mind. I know that I am better focused; I can remember better; I am performing better."

If each user were to undertake a similar experiment in a conscientious way, I believe he would come to the same conclusion and would gain personal insight into the drug's effects upon him that would tally with what scientists are finding through their own clinical observations and medical research.

Dr. Hardin B. Jones
Professor of Medical Physics and Physiology
University of California, Berkeley
October, 1976

*Jones, H. B. and Jones, H. C. (1977). *Sensual Drugs: Deprivation and Rehabilitation of the Mind.* Cambridge University Press, New York, Cambridge and Sydney.

Cannabis Sativa: Background Information

Cannabis sativa, more commonly known as marihuana, Indian hemp, or hashish, is an annual, herbaceous plant and has been cultivated for centuries as a source of fiber for making rope, for the oil content of its seed and, more recently, for the intoxicating substances found in its flowering tops. In many parts of the world the plant grows as a weed and exhibits extremely rapid growth, similar to the hops plant, a related species.

There is a wide variety of cannabis preparations, depending upon the region of the world in which it is grown and used. For the most part, marihuana for use as an intoxicant is prepared from dried mature leaves, dried flowering tops and, in some cases, the entire dried plant. It is usually smoked.

Before 1964, the intoxicating properties of marihuana could not be related to a specific chemical constituent of the plant. In the past 14 years, however, the complex chemistry of marihuana has been elucidated and much information is now available. The principal psychoactive ingredient is known to be delta-9-tetra-hydrocannabinol (delta-9-THC), although there are at least 50 identifiable substances present. Other constituents include delta-8-THC, cannabinol (CBN), and cannabadiol (CBD).

The identification of delta-9-THC in 1964 was the first significant breakthrough in the study of cannabis and represented an achievement similar to the isolation of morphine from the opium poppy, cocaine from coca leaves and mescaline from the peyote cactus. The identification of delta-9-THC as the principal psychoactive component has enabled the pharmacologist and the biochemist to assess quantitatively marihuana's mode of action. Much of the early work dealing with cannabis was conducted with material that had not been assayed for active ingredients or had not been stored under optimal conditions, especially as THC is rapidly inactivated by exposure to oxygen, light, humidity and elevated temperature.

Two main types of *Cannabis sativa* have been defined according to the concentration of THC contained in their flowering tops. The fiber-type plant has low THC content (less than 0.2%), and the drug-type plant has a high THC content (1% to 7%). A 1-gram cigarette of the drug type, therefore, contains 10 to 70 milligrams of THC. Sources of cannabis found to be low in THC concentration contain high amounts of CBD and other cannabinoids.

The intake of 5 to 10 milligrams of delta-9-THC into the bloodsteam is held to be sufficient to induce cannabis intoxication. Allowing for the inefficiency of inhalation, one can readily see that a single marihuana cigarette of the drug type is sufficient to induce a marihuana "high." A great deal of the marihuana consumed in the United States before 1970 was relatively weak and contained less than 1% THC. Much of the currently available marihuana comes from Jamaica, Mexico and Colombia and has an estimated content of 3 to 4% THC, an extremely potent dosage.

Hashish is a more concentrated preparation of resinous material found in the flowering tops of *Cannabis sativa,* and may contain as much as 10% THC. Liquid hashish or "marihuana oil" with a potency of 30 to 90% THC is also available and has been characterized as "one of the most frightening drugs on the market today."[67]

As defined by the National Commission on Marihuana in 1972, the following terms apply to the use of cannabis: *Intermittent* users employ the drug from twice a month to once a week; *moderate* users, once a week to daily; *heavy* (chronic) users, once to several times daily.

Marihuana Today

1. Introduction

Ten or twelve years ago when the use of drugs became increasingly prevalent on college campuses in this country, many of my students asked my opinion about marihuana. At that time, without more scientific evidence at my disposal, I could not pretend to speak factually about the effects of this subtle and complex drug on the human mind and on the various aspects of bodily health. I did urge my science students, however, to bear in mind that among pharmacologists there is general agreement that a drug must be presumed harmful until proven otherwise.

In order to respond to my students' questions in a responsible and scientific manner I subsequently undertook a thorough survey of the medical literature. The many scientific journals that I studied showed a solid body of clinical and experimental data warranting an extremely cautious approach to the drug. In reviewing these data I was struck by the fact that almost none of this information had reached the general public, and that, as a result, many held marihuana to be harmless.

To bridge the communications gap that clearly exists between the scientific community and the public, a clear summary of recent findings seemed in order, detailed enough to present a meaningful picture, but short enough to be readily understandable. In the following article, I have tried to provide such a summary, both for my students and for the many others who are seriously concerned about the effects of this drug.

Since 1969, when the Federal Government began making marihuana of controlled quality available to research scientists, reliable evidence of marihuana's effects has accumulated at a rapid pace. These nine years of research have provided strong indications that the drug in its various forms is far more hazardous than was originally suspected. In fact, eminent scientists from around the world agree that, based on recent findings, marihuana must be considered a very dangerous drug.

Available findings suggest that the effects of marihuana are cumulative and dose-related, and that prolonged use of marihuana, or less frequent use of the more potent hashish, is associated with at least six different types of hazards. Senator Eastland, Chairman of the Internal Security Subcommittee of the United States Senate, summarized testimony given before the Subcommittee in May, 1974, by a distinguished body of internationally-known medical researchers in the following way:

1)—THC, the principal psychoactive factor in cannabis, tends to accumulate in the brain and gonads and other fatty tissues in the manner of DDT. . . .

2)—Marihuana, even when used in moderate amounts, causes damage to the entire cellular process. . . .

3)—Tied in with its tendency to accumulate in the brain and its capacity for cellular damage, there is a growing body of evidence that marihuana inflicts irreversible damage on the brain, including actual brain atrophy, when used in a chronic manner for several years. . . .

4)—There is also a growing body of evidence that marihuana adversely affects the reproductive process in a number of ways, and that it poses a serious danger of genetic damage and even of genetic mutation. . . .

5)—Chronic cannabis smoking can produce sinusitis, pharyngitis, bronchitis, emphysema and other respiratory difficulties in a year or less, as opposed to ten or twenty years of cigarette smoking to produce comparable complications. . . .

6)—Cannabis smoke, or cannabis smoke mixed with cigarette smoke, is far more damaging to lung tissues than tobacco smoke alone. The damage done is described as "precancerous.". . .

7)—Chronic cannabis use results in deterioration of mental functioning, pathological forms of thinking resembling paranoia, and a "massive and chronic passivity" and lack of motivation—the so-called "amotivational syndrome.". . .[65]

There can be no doubt that in the past few years this country has been caught in a cannabis epidemic. The amount of marihuana seized by federal authorities has risen from 85,715 pounds in 1968 to 783,000 pounds in 1973; similarly, the amount of hashish seized has escalated from 534 pounds in 1968 to 53,000 pounds in 1973. These are alarming quantities when you consider that a pound of marihuana can intoxicate almost 200 people, while a pound of hashish can intoxicate eight times as many. Moreover, officials estimate that roughly eight pounds of each drug reaches users for every one pound seized. Thus, close to 7 million pounds of marihuana and hashish may have been consumed in the United States in 1973—enough to make more than 2 billion cigarettes! In 1974, the amount of marihuana that federal authorities seized jumped almost threefold over the previous year to 2,009,000 pounds—a startling rise for a one-year period—while the amount of hashish decreased slightly to 51,000 pounds.[67] In 1977, the Drug Enforcement Administration is reported to have seized approximately three million pounds of marihuana, an extraordinary increase from previous years.

This massive escalation in the quantities of marihuana and hashish consumed has been paralleled by a continuing escalation in the potency of cannabis preparations since the mid-1960s. Before 1970, most of the marihuana consumed in this country was of domestic origin, which is low in THC content—1/5 of 1% and under.[109] This fact among others would help to explain why many observers in the early years came to the conclusion that it was not seriously damaging. By 1970, Mexican marihuana had replaced the domestic variety, and enjoyed a virtual monopoly in the American market over the next few years. The average potency of the Mexican marihuana entering the country during this time is estimated to have been between 1.5 and 2% THC.[109] Around the end of 1973, Jamaican, Mexican and Colombian marihuana, with an estimated potency of 3 to 4% entered this country in increasing quantities.[45] In addition, federal authorities began to seize increasing amounts of liquid hashish or "marihuana oil" with a potency ranging from 30 to 90% THC. At an average potency of 50% THC, an ounce of "oil" is enough to intoxicate over 1,000 people. In 1974, 369 pounds were seized.[45]

Commenting on the tremendous increase in both the quantity and potency of cannabis imports into the United States, Andrew C. Tartaglino, Acting Deputy Administrator of the Drug Enforcement Administration, told the Senate Subcommittee Hearing that: "The traffic in and abuse of marihuana products has taken a more serious turn in the last two or three years than either the courts, the news media, or the public is aware. The shift is clearly toward the abuse of stronger, more dangerous forms of the drug, which renders much of what has been said in the 1960s about the harmlessness of its use obsolete."[105]

At a 1975 Hearing before the same Senate Subcommittee, Dr. Robert L. DuPont, then Director of the National Institute on Drug Abuse, cited new evidence of the use of marihuana by large numbers of very young individuals.

> A 1974 survey found that in one high-use county in California, 22 percent of the seventh grade boys and 18 percent of seventh grade girls reported having used marihuana at least once during the preceding year; and that its use with 11th and 12th grade boys exceeded that of tobacco. A survey of a national sample of 23-year-old men in 1974 found that almost 10 percent reported smoking marihuana daily during the preceding year. In this group, the daily use of marihuana grew from under 3 percent 4 years earlier and nearly equalled the daily use of alcohol, which was 14 percent. . . .[16]

Drug Use Among American High School Students 1975-1977, a survey conducted by the Institute for Social Research at the University of Michigan, reported evidence of the use of marihuana by large numbers of very young individuals. It states:

> Marihuana is by far the most widely used illicit drug with 56% [high school seniors] reporting some use in their lifetime, 48% reporting some use in the past year, and 35% use in the past month.[45a]
> Marihuana has shown a marked increase in the proportion using it (and/or hashish) daily. The proportion reporting daily use in the class of 1975 (6.0%) came as a surprise to many.

However, since then the number has risen considerably, so that now *one in every eleven high school seniors (9.1%) indicates that he or she uses the drug on a daily or near daily basis* (emphasis added).[45a]
There has been a substantial and continuing increase in the prevalence of early use. In the class of 1975, only 17% reported use prior to tenth grade, vs. 22% of the class of 1976 and 26% of the class of 1977.[45a]

Dr. DuPont commented that these trends, which show that a large and growing minority use the drug more frequently, at a higher potency and at a younger age, disturb "even the most optimistic observers of the contemporary marihuana scene in this country."[16] He adds that medical findings of the past several years raise "doubts about the harmlessness of smoking marihuana even in low doses."[16] It is revealing to note that the Michigan University survey shows that "the great majority of students (at least two of every three) perceive regular use of any of the illicit drugs to entail "great risk" of harm for the users, with the single exception of marihuana."[45a]

Also significant and, according to DuPont, "one of the saddest lessons of the last few years" is the fact that "there is not a tradeoff between marihuana and alcohol" as many once thought. "Parents would say, 'Well, if Johnny is smoking grass, he will not be drinking booze'. Unfortunately, the evidence is exactly the contrary. We have found that these behaviors are linked behaviors, so that the consumption of any substance, licit or illicit, is positively correlated with an increased consumption of all other substances."[16]

One of the major factors that has encouraged widespread use of marihuana has been the one-sided publicity given statements of scientists and lay spokesmen advocating a more tolerant attitude toward the drug. Conversely, there has been a virtual blackout, until recently, of scientific writings pointing to its dangers. In a recent report Keith Cowan, advisor to various Canadian provincial governments and consultant on drug education, commented on the one-sided treatment of the cannabis issue:

The sad truth is that highly important and cautionary evidence has been available for years in the literature and in the experience of prominent medical men who have treated cannabis habitués. But it has not reached our youth and the public in any effective way as yet. . . . On a recent trip to England I searched bookstores associated with the University of London and the University of Oxford. Excepting one book, the only books openly available gave cannabis a basically clean bill of health. One document stated succinctly that science had not established that marihuana was as harmful as tobacco. . . . Visits to five other universities on the U.S. eastern seaboard brought the communication gap home even more seriously. In one major university, I thoroughly investigated the literature in the bookstores, and every single drug study was favorable to cannabis. The dean of students told me that while they were observing ill effects on students using the drug in increasing numbers, they had no confirmation in the general literature and were therefore silent.[13]

Thus, books like Lester Grinspoon's *Marihuana Reconsidered*[25] and the Consumers Union's *Licit and Illicit Drugs*,[5] both of which took the stand that marihuana was not seriously dangerous and could therefore be legalized, received favorable reviews and the authors were invited to appear on numerous television talk shows. In contrast, the book *Marihuana — Deceptive Weed*[77] by Gabriel G. Nahas, a distinguished medical scientist with numerous publications and a long-standing reputation, was ignored, although it had been presented to the appropriate press and magazine outlets with excellent references by numerous scientific authorities. Also ignored were the warnings concerning marihuana's potential harm made in 1972 by Dr. Olav J. Braenden, Director of the United Nations Narcotics Laboratory in Geneva. Based on his own experience and the experience of 26 cooperating laboratories in various parts of the world, Braenden stated that there was a general consensus among scientists working in the field that marihuana is a dangerous drug.[4]

Another case in point is the publicity surrounding the first report of the National Commission on Marihuana and Drug Abuse. According to Dr. Henry Brill, one of the Commission members, many misinterpretations resulted from stressing reassuring passages in the report and ignoring the final conclusions and recommendations, as well as the passages in the report on which they were based:

18

From my knowledge of the proceedings of the Commission, I can reaffirm that the report and the subsequent statements by the Commission meant exactly what they said, namely, that the drug should not be legalized, that control measures for trafficking in the drug were necessary and should be continued, and that use of this drug should be discouraged because of its potential hazards. . . .
Scientific reports which have become available since the report was written confirm still further the need for caution. . . . In general the effects of the drug continue to be noted as subtle and insidious. . . . I may add that in my own view marihuana must still be classed as a dangerous drug, dangerous to enough people to warrant full control.[7]

Because of this strange imbalance in publicity, intelligent people have been under the impression that the bulk of the scientific community considers marihuana to be innocuous. This is not so. Many scientists are coming forward with significant data attesting to the drug's adverse effects, and many of their findings overlap and mutually support one another. In addition to Drs. Braenden and Nahas, these scientists include Professor W.D.M. Paton of Oxford University, who heads the British drug research program and is one of the world's leading pharmacologists; Professor Nils Bejerot of Sweden, perhaps the ranking international expert on the epidemiology of drug abuse; Professor M.I. Soueif of Egypt, author of the classic study on the consequences of hashish addiction in his country; Professor Robert G. Heath, Chairman of the Department of Psychiatry and Neurology at Tulane University Medical School; Professor Morton A. Stenchever, Chairman of the Department of Obstetrics and Gynecology at the University of Utah Medical School; Dr. Julius Axelrod, Nobel Prize winning researcher of the National Institute of Mental Health; the late Dr. Hardin B. Jones, Professor of Medical Physics and Physiology at the University of California, Berkeley; Dr. D. Harvey Powelson, head of the Psychiatric Division of the Student Health Service at Berkeley between 1964 and 1972; Dr. Henry Brill, senior psychiatric member of the National Commission on Marihuana and President of the American Psychopathological Association; and others.

It is significant that two of these men, Heath and Powelson, had once leaned toward a tolerant attitude on marihuana, but were later compelled by their findings to revise their views. Thus,

19

although Heath originally shared the belief that marihuana was a relatively innocent drug producing relaxation with no significant side-effects, he has since concluded that it is highly dangerous.[34] Powelson, whose extensive exposure at Berkeley over eight years makes him probably the most experienced campus psychiatrist in the country, has said that when the marihuana epidemic first broke in 1965 and 1966, he had adopted a lenient stance toward the drug, based on the then almost universal assumption that marihuana was not seriously harmful. As a result of his extensive clinical experience, however, his attitude toward marihuana has changed to the point that he now considers it the most dangerous drug with which the United States must contend. Powelson summarized the psychological effects of cannabis in the following way:

> 1)—Its early use is beguiling. It gives the illusion of feeling good. The user is not aware of the beginning loss of mental functioning. I have never seen an exception to the observation that marihuana impairs the user's ability to judge the loss of his own mental functioning.
> 2)—After one to three years of continuous use the ability to think has become so impaired that pathological forms of thinking begin to take over the entire thought process.
> 3)—Chronic heavy use leads to paranoid thinking.
> 4)—Chronic heavy use leads to deterioration in body and mental functioning which is difficult and perhaps impossible to reverse.
> 5)—Its use leads to a delusional system of thinking which has inherent in it the strong need to seduce and proselytize others. I have rarely seen a regular marihuana user who wasn't "pushing." As these people move into government, the professions, and the media, it is not surprising that they continue as "pushers," thus adding to the confusion that [the scientific community is obliged] to ameliorate.[87]

The following sections will consider the specific ways in which cannabis affects mental and physical health. It is perhaps fitting to begin with a review of some of the first experimental work with delta-9-THC, and of the controversy that has surrounded the marihuana question ever since. The point at issue was then, and is still, whether marihuana should be deemed a soft recreational drug, or whether it must be regarded as a dangerous substance calling for strict control.

2. Mild Intoxicant or Hallucinogenic Drug?

The first experimental study with pure delta-9-THC was made in 1967 by Dr. Harris Isbell and colleagues of the University of Kentucky Medical Center, who showed that the physical and psychological effects of cannabis were related to the dose administered; they confirmed the older observations of the French physician, Jacques Moreau,[72] concerning the hallucinogenic properties of the drug. Isbell concluded his study as follows: "The data in our experiments definitely indicate that the psychotomimetic* effects of delta-9-THC are dependent on dosage and that sufficiently high doses (15-20 mg. smoked, 20-60 mg. ingested) can cause psychotic reactions in any individual."[43] Isbell classified cannabis among the hallucinogens.

On the other hand, studies by Dr. Andrew T. Weil of Harvard Medical School[110] and by Alfred Crancer, Jr. and colleagues[14] indicated that cannabis was a "mild intoxicant" which produced effects not related to dosage and which did not impair, and in certain instances even improved, the performance of chronic users in selected tests.

With the publication of these three studies, the great marihuana debate in the United States began. Is cannabis a hallucinogen? Or is it a mild intoxicant when used in a dosage likely to be taken by habitual users in the population at large? In coming to terms with this crucial question, it will be necessary to scrutinize the evidence supporting the two contradictory positions.

The laboratory study conducted by Weil made use of marihuana cigarettes containing what were thought to be doses of 4.5 to 18 mg. of delta-9-THC. In this study non-users smoking marihuana for the first time experienced a few subjective effects, demonstrated impaired performance on simple intellectual and manual dexterity tests, showed moderate acceleration of heart-beat (not dose-related) and exhibited reddening of the eyes. Experienced marihuana users exhibited increases in heart rate higher than those observed in non-users (also not dose-related), reported a subjective "high," and showed slight improvement of their performance on the tests.

On the basis of these observations, Weil concluded that "marihuana is a relatively mild intoxicant."[110] [111] Weil's paper was

*Capable of inducing altered states of consciousness.

21

published in *Science* magazine, was extensively quoted in an article on marihuana in *Scientific American* by the Harvard psychiatrist, Lester Grinspoon,[24] and was the subject of a feature article on the front page of the *New York Times*. His paper, with the attendant publicity it received, was read by many and contributed to the widely held belief in the United States that marihuana is a relatively harmless substance with few untoward effects.

It is now apparent that the actual dose of psychoactive material absorbed by the subjects in the Weil study must have been quite low. All subsequent studies by other investigators in which the delta-9-THC concentration was accurately measured indicate that the doses purportedly used by Weil produce much more significant impairment of psychomotor performance and much greater dose-dependent increases in heart rate. Weil's cannabis, inadequately assayed for THC content, had probably undergone considerable decay due to the well-known instability of THC between the time of preparation and its actual use in his experiments. In commenting on this point, Dr. Leo E. Hollister of the Veterans Administration Hospital, Palo Alto, California, reported that many of his own cannabis samples had only 10% of the alleged THC content, under conditions of aging similar to Weil's.[39]

A similar criticism can be made of the simulated driving study of Crancer, also published in *Science* and quoted in part in *Scientific American*. Driving skills of volunteer subjects were tested with a driving simulator after the volunteers had consumed large amounts of alcohol or had smoked two marihuana cigarettes containing supposed doses of 22 mg. delta-9-THC. In the studies of Isbell reported two years earlier, an actual assayed dose of this amount produced "hallucinations, depersonalization, and derealization."[43] In the Crancer study, under conditions of supposed marihuana intoxication, speedometer errors were increased (the subjects did not watch the speedometer carefully), but driving ability was not otherwise impaired. Acceleration, braking, signalling, steering and total errors were unaffected. In contrast, profound impairment was observed with the large doses of alcohol administered. Crancer concluded that "impairment in simulated driving performance is not a function of increased marihuana dosage or inexperience with the drug."[14] He did not discuss the discrepancy between his study and that of Isbell. However, he was careful *not* to state that the use of marihuana will not impair actual driving on the highway, or that it is safer to use than alcohol.

But some of the readers of his paper were less cautious. Grinspoon, discussing the Crancer paper, stated, "It was found that marihuana causes significantly less impairment of driving ability than alcohol does."[24] Grinspoon also relied heavily on the studies of Weil and Crancer in his book *Marihuana Reconsidered,* where he asserted that, "if an habitual or relatively frequent user had a specific task to carry out, he would be able to do so as effectively while experiencing a 'social marihuana high' as he would if he were entirely drug-free, and in some cases he may perform more efficiently or accurately."[25] This book was hailed by the *New York Times Book Review* as presenting "the best dope on pot so far."

In his pioneering study of the effects of delta-9-THC on human subjects, Isbell used chemically prepared and assayed material. Doses of 4 and 18 mg. smoked, or 8 to 35 mg. ingested, were accompanied by marked distortion of visual and auditory perception, lost sense of reality, depersonalization and, in some instances, hallucinations. Isbell also found that the physical and psychological changes experienced by each subject were directly proportional to the amount of THC consumed.

The observations of Isbell on the adverse effects of delta-9-THC on mental performance have been substantiated by subsequent well-controlled studies,[20] whose findings cast still more doubt on the validity of the results described by Weil and Crancer. One such example is the careful, well-controlled study undertaken in 1974 of driving in city traffic after smoking both high and low doses of marihuana.[51] This study showed that the drug had a dose-dependent adverse effect on driving performance. Forty-two percent of those on low doses (4.9 mg. THC per cigarette) and 63% of those on high doses (8.4 mg. THC per cigarette) showed a decline in their driving ability after smoking one marihuana cigarette. Unusual behavior included "the missing of traffic lights or stop signs; . . . passing maneuvers without sufficient caution; poor anticipation or poor handling of vehicle with respect to traffic flow; [and] unawareness or inappropriate awareness of pedestrians or stationary vehicles...."[51] The use of marihuana in conjunction with alcohol was also shown to reinforce the adverse effects on performance of some motor tasks.[65] Other studies confirm that marihuana definitely impairs driving ability.[37] An increase in the accident rate among marihuana users is also beginning to show up in the records of emergency treatment centers.[45]

It is probable that the absence of untoward effects of cannabis reported in the studies of Weil and Crancer was caused by the highly reduced amounts of delta-9-THC in the material they used. Unlike Isbell and others, each failed to assay his material accurately by independently-calibrated techniques at the time of the actual experiment.

Weil and Crancer published their findings in 1968 and 1969. Their papers are by no means the only or the most recent contributions to the exculpatory literature. I have already mentioned Grinspoon's *Marihuana Reconsidered,* and *Licit and Illicit Drugs* by Edward M. Brecher and the editors of *Consumer Reports.* In the March 1975 issue of *Consumer Reports,* Brecher returns to the subject with an article entitled *Marijuana: The Health Questions;*[6] and another quite similar article by the Harvard psychiatrist, Dr. Norman E. Zinberg, appeared in *Psychology Today* (Dec., 1976),[118] a publication with very wide circulation among college undergraduates. Both articles review the case against marihuana, and then go on to cite contradictory evidence that seemingly gives the lie to many of the conclusions reached by the Senate Internal Security Subcommittee on the basis of the testimony presented before it. Brecher does not assert that marihuana is harmless; on the contrary, "no drug is safe or harmless to all people at all dosage levels or under all conditions of use."[6] But out of all the available evidence, he believes,

> . . . a general pattern is beginning to emerge. When a research finding can be readily checked — either by repeating the experiment or by devising a better one — an allegation of adverse marijuana effects is relatively short-lived. No damage is found — and after a time the allegation is dropped (often to be replaced by allegations of some other kind of damage due to marijuana).[6]

The evidence Brecher marshalls in support of this contention comes from a number of different sources. Key to his argument, however, is the so-called Jamaica study.[93] Zinberg also cites this study often and characterizes it as "a splendid piece of anthropological research."[118] Reasoning that effects of marihuana consumption predicted in this country on the basis of laboratory research should be readily evident in societies that have used cannabis for generations, the National Institute of Mental Health in 1970 commissioned the Research Institute for the Study of Man to study marihuana use on the island of Jamaica. Marihuana, or ganja as it is known there, was introduced into Jamaica in the 17th century as a possible source of fiber. It is estimated that something under ten percent of the population uses ganja regularly, either in cigarettes or as tea.[28]

Following a period of research in the field, the six anthropologists who conducted the study selected a group of 30 ganja smokers and a control group of 30 non-smokers to undergo physical and psychological testing at University Hospital of the University of the West Indies. The tests included lung X-rays, brain-wave recordings, chromosome studies, and a battery of psychiatric and psychological examinations aimed at uncovering evidence of emotional disturbance or brain damage. No significant differences were found between the ganja users and the controls, leading the researchers to give marihuana the nearest thing to a clean bill of health.

Taken at face value, those are certainly impressive findings. But how do they agree with the findings of others who have had extensive clinical experience in Jamaica? In his testimony before the Senate Subcommittee on Internal Security Dr. Henry Brill, a member of the National Commission on Marihuana and Drug Abuse, drew attention to the conflicting evidence from Jamaica:

> Finally, one should note the comment from Jamaica in the West Indies where the effects of cannabis had been thought to be relatively benign; among the middle class it is now found to be associated with school dropouts, transient psychoses, panic states, and adolescent behavior disorders. In general the effects of the drug continue to be noted as subtle and insidious.[7]

Dr. John A.S. Hall, since 1965 Chairman of the Department of Medicine at Kingston Hospital, Jamaica, has had unparalleled opportunity for first-hand observation. He reports:

1)—An emphysema-bronchitis syndrome, common among Indian laborers of a past generation, who were well known for their ganja smoking habits, is now a well-established present day finding among black male laborers [in Jamaica].

2)—Ganja has long been regarded both by the laity and the profession as a cause of psychosis in Jamaica. The unrivaled, accumulated experience of Cooke, Royes, and Williams, who were in recent years senior medical officers at Bellevue Hospital, in Kingston, Jamaica, fully substantiate this.

3)—An incidence of 20 percent impotence as a presenting feature among males who have smoked ganja for 5 or more years, was reported by me earlier.

4)—Personality changes among ganja smokers and members of the Rastafari cult are a matter of common observation in Jamaica. The apathy, the retreat from reality, the incapacity or unwillingness for sustained concentration, and the lifetime of drifting are best summed up in the "amotivational syndrome" of McGlothin & West.[23]

When confronted with conflicting evidence of such proportions, the conscientious reporter digs deeper. He then soon discovers that the Jamaica study suffered from numerous scientific-methodological shortcomings. The chromosome study technique, for instance, was so deficient that 27 of the 60 cell cultures did not grow at all and could not be scored; other methodological deficiencies were so extensive as to render the results meaningless. Standard lung X-rays are an important diagnostic test for many pulmonary disorders, but they do not reveal the emphysema-bronchitis syndrome which has been so widely attributed to heavy marihuana use. And, as we shall see later, it has already been clearly established that the standard scalp electroencephalograms that were taken during the Jamaica study are incapable of detecting the cannabis-induced brainwave abnormalities that have been recorded by electrodes implanted deep within the brain.

When he was asked to comment on the seemingly paradoxical results of the Jamaica study, Hall had this to say:

The study to which you refer does not have the general support of experienced clinicians and other workers in the field. We believe that the selection with which the study was done was faulty and that in regard to the reported absence of any change in the chromosome pattern that their technique was faulty and that certainly as regards the statement that there was no respiratory effect, it is unfounded.[28]

In his article, Brecher makes much of the difficulty he encountered in obtaining a copy of the Jamaica study report. The report has not been released by the sponsoring government agency, and Consumers Union finally secured a copy from Holland. Perhaps the explanation for this so extraordinary unavailability is to be found in the value placed on the study by those who, like Dr. Hall, have the professional qualifications to assess its worth.

3. The Psyche

The psychological effects of chronic marihuana consumption are familiar to most clinicans who have treated cannabis users and, for that matter, to lay observers who have had extended acquaintance with cannabis habitués. These effects have perhaps been best described by Drs. Harold Kolansky and William T. Moore, two Philadelphia psychiatrists affiliated with the University of Pennsylvania, who conducted one of the first well-documented studies of the effects of cannabis on the human psyche.

Between 1965 and 1974, Kolansky and Moore treated hundreds of patients where the use of marihuana was in the foreground of the clinical picture. They described their findings with 51 of these patients in several publications. A 1971 report in the Journal of the American Medical Association[53] dealt with 38 young people ranging in age from 13 to 24 years, all of whom smoked marihuana two or more times weekly, and in general smoked two or more marihuana cigarettes each time, and all of whom showed adverse psychological symptoms. In a follow-up study of an older group, Kolansky and Moore examined 13 adults from 20 to 41 years of age, all of whom smoked cannabis products intensively (three to ten times per week) for a period of 16 months to 6 years.[54]

As their purpose was to determine the impact of cannabis on the psyche, those included in the studies were carefully screened. The mental status of each prior to cannabis use was established by means of a thorough psychiatric history. Anyone who had displayed psychological problems before smoking cannabis was eliminated; only those were retained in whom no evidence was found of a predisposition to mental illness prior to the development of psychopathological symptoms once the smoking of cannabis had begun. It was also ascertained that these individuals had used only marihuana and/or hashish to the exclusion of other drugs—with the exception of five from the older group who had used additional drugs, but to such a limited extent that it was unlikely to account for their symptomology.

According to Kolansky amd Moore, "marihuana and hashish have a chemical effect that produces a brain syndrome marked by distortion of perception and reality."[71] They have summarized their findings as follows:

During the past six years, we have seen a clinical entity different from the routine syndromes usually seen in adolescents and young adults. Long and careful diagnostic evaluation convinced us that this entity is a toxic reaction in the central nervous system due to regular use of marihuana and hashish. Contrary to what is frequently reported, we have found the effect not merely that of a mild intoxicant which causes a mild exaggeration of usual adolescent behavior, but a *specific* and *separate* clinical syndrome unlike any other variation of the abnormal manifestations of adolescence. We feel there should be no confusion, because regardless of the underlying psychological difficulty, mental changes—hallmarked by disturbed awareness of the self, apathy, confusion, and poor reality testing—will occur in an individual who smokes marihuana on a regular basis whether he is a normal adolescent, an adolescent in conflict, or a severely neurotic individual.[52]

The most striking feature of Kolansky and Moore's studies—and a feature corroborated by the experience of other clinicians—was the uniformity of the symptoms they observed. Mental confusion, inability to concentrate, diminished attention span, loss of will power, and difficulties with concept formation and recent memory, were common symptoms. The patients often displayed a goallessness or serious loss of motivation. Paranoid suspiciousness of others and regression to a more infantile state were also common, especially among the adolescent patients. In many patients of high school age, steadily declining academic ability and class standing were common and were in direct proportion to the frequency and amount of smoking.

Three case histories illustrate many of these points:

A 20-year-old college student was referred by her family physician because of a marked and relatively sudden change in behavior and life style. She had been an outstanding history major until the previous year when she gave up living with a roommate, lived as a recluse, stopped attending classes regularly, did not turn in assignments, frequently spent days in bed, appeared apathetic, confused, withdrawn, and asocial. She often had periods of marked depression, felt there was no purpose in school life and gave up her history major, shifting her interest to economics, music, and then art. In each field, she failed to study or produce and had strong wishes to drop out of school and live in a commune.

During psychiatric examination she was lethargic, had difficulty concentrating, had trouble with memory and attention span, and spoke of long periods of depression and sleeplessness. She had aimless relations with her former friends and had no greater ambition "than to turn on with a joint." She moved slowly and without purpose and had frequent headaches. Her symptom complex had begun within months of beginning to smoke marihuana first on weekends and then two or three times each week. At the time of referral she was smoking four times each week. A review of the absence of symptoms prior to the use of cannabis, the correlation of her apathetic withdrawal from responsibility, and her thinking disorder with the onset of cannabis use motivated her to try to give up using marihuana and within two months her smoking stopped. Within weeks after that, much of the confusion, apathy, and poor memory had disappeared. She returned to college, on a more limited basis, and gradually had a return of interest. At the time of this writing, it was not yet six months after cessation of cannabis use but she had had a recovery to most of her precannabis-smoking personality. She had used amphetamines on three occasions early in the period when she began marihuana use but had given these up because her gratification with marihuana was more intense.[54]

A 19-year-old boy entered college with an "A" average. He began smoking marihuana early in the freshman year, and within two months of starting to smoke cannabis, he became apathetic, disoriented, and depressed. At the semester's end, he had failed all courses and lacked judgment in most other matters. Upon return to his home, he discontinued marihuana after a total period of three and a half months of smoking. Gradually, his apathy disappeared, his motivation returned, and his personal appearance improved. He found employment, and in the following academic year, he enrolled at a different university as a preprofessional student. His motivation returned, as did his capability. As with so many of our patients, this young man told his psychiatrist that he had observed changes while smoking marihuana; he even went to a college counselor and told the counselor that he felt he was having a thinking problem due to smoking marihuana. The counselor reassured him that the drug was harmless and that there was no medical evidence of difficulties as a consequence of smoking.[54]

A 28-year-old white schoolteacher smoked marihuana and hashish for six years. He admitted to the use of LSD on three occasions, each accompanied by a typical "acid trip" early in his drug history, the last of which caused such terror as to make him stop using it. He began smoking marihuana while he was a college senior. Over the next few years he progressed from weekend smoking to using the drug three to four times per week. As a teacher in a boys' boarding school he spent a great deal of his spare time with the students discussing philosophy and politics. When it was discovered that he had encouraged students to smoke marihuana he was in trouble with the school administration. Finally his advocacy of the violent overthrow of the government resulted in his dismissal. Shortly afterward he obtained a position at another private school and within the year had repeated his earlier experience. In addition, he developed a disinterest in sexual relations with his wife and became interested in "depth philosophy" which he understood rather poorly. His estrangement from reality became more obvious to all. When he was prevailed upon to withdraw from marihuana use, a minimal return to his previous personality occurred, but the remission was still not complete after eight months. Even though his cognitive thinking was more sensible and he seemed to be more firmly rooted in reality, he still complained of difficulty with concentration and sometimes during conversations he had a tendency to forget the content of his statements.[54]

As a result of cannabis use, emotional disorders also seem to develop. Among patients examined by Kolansky and Moore, a considerable "flattening of affect" gave a "false impression of calm and well-being; this was usually accompanied by the patients' conviction that they had recently developed emotional maturity and insight aided by cannabis. This pseudo-equanimity was easily disrupted, however, if the patients were questioned about their personality change, new philosophy, and drug consumption; or if their supplies of cannabis were threatened,"[53] so that irritability and outbursts of aggression were not uncommon. Many also showed an impairment in the control of their own impulses and judgment, and an inability to distinguish the subtleties of the feelings of others in social situations. Moreover, most of the patients admitted to a growing sense of isolation from others and a desire to shun social activities, as well as a deep-seated feeling of anxiety and depression. It should be noted that the severity of the symptoms varied greatly in different individuals. Thus, 8 of the 38 young patients suffered from marked psychosis, while 6 others suffered a milder form of ego decompensation. Symptoms ranged in effect from mild ego disturbance to severe psychosis in individuals who showed no ego fragility, predisposition toward psychosis, or other abnormal tendencies prior to taking marihuana. Suicide was actually attempted by four of the most seriously disturbed. It appears characteristic of cannabis use that the severity of its effect is unpredictable and that an acute psychotic reaction can occur in a mentally healthy individual from even a single dose.[10]

In many patients, the tendency toward magical thinking and an altered sense of reality was observed, and this often included symptoms of paranoia. Two rather extreme case histories illustrate this point:

> A 16-year-old girl in whom there was no prior psychiatric difficulty smoked cannabis derivatives (marihuana and hashish) at first occasionally, and then three to four times weekly for a period of two years. She began to lose interest in academic work and became preoccupied with political issues. From a quiet and socially popular girl, she became hostile and quite impulsive in her inappropriate verbal attacks on teachers and peers. She dropped out of school in her senior year of high school, which led to psychiatric referral. She showed inappropriate affect and developed paranoid ideas about an older sister's husband having sexual interests in her. She refused to give up smoking marihuana and eventually became so depressed that she attempted suicide by hanging. After withdrawal from the drug, her depression and paranoid ideas slowly disappeared, as did her outbursts of aggression. Ten months of follow-up showed continued impairment of memory and thought disorder, marked by her complaint that she could not concentrate on her studies and could not transform her thoughts into either written or spoken words as she had once been able to do quite easily.[53]

> A married 24-year-old man who had shown no previous psychiatric illness or evidence of personality disorder met a group of new friends who taught him to smoke marihuana. He enjoyed the experience so much that he smoked it daily for two months, claiming it did not interfere with his daily functioning. He even said that he could think more clearly. Gradually he began to withdraw from his friends and seemed suspicious of them. He developed ideas of reference, believing that his friends talked about him saying that he was impotent. (Impotence had actually occurred on several occasions after he had smoked a

large amount of "good hash.") He also believed he was developing heart disease as a result of "bad drugs." He had experienced palpitations and a feeling of his heart "jumping" in his throat on several occasions while smoking some Mexican marihuana. He believed that his friends were trying to do away with him in order to have his wife. At the end of two months, he showed a full-blown paranoid psychosis and had delusions of grandeur. He believed that he had developed a superior intellect at the expense of a loss of his sexual life. He was the first member of a new "super race." After stopping his smoking his delusional ideas disappeared and he returned to his normal functioning in his job and marriage.[53]

According to Kolansky and Moore, many of the long-term marihuana smokers who develop paranoid delusions appear able to function for a period of time "without others being aware of their illness, either because they join groups who share their aberrational thinking or because they keep their delusional thoughts to themselves."[53]

In the course of their research, Kolansky amd Moore established the fact that the symptoms demonstrated by their patients began with cannabis use and disappeared or were reduced within 3 to 24 months of abstention from the drug. This, coupled with the stereotypical nature of these symptoms, led them to hypothesize that the psychic changes they observed were actually caused by physical ones — the direct or indirect chemical effect of cannabis on the brain. They suggested that a toxic agent — cannabis — produced transient biochemical changes in the central nervous system, quite possibly in the cerebral cortex, and that these, in turn, produced the symptoms of psychic aberration typical of cannabis use. This subject is examined in greater detail in the next section.

While Kolansky and Moore were among the first to take issue with the widely-held view that marihuana is a mild intoxicant causing serious psychological disturbances only in rare cases, they are by no means the only clinicians to have done so. Others have corroborated their observations in independent studies, and have come to similar conclusions. Among them are Dr. Hardin B. Jones of Berkeley and Dr. Leo Hollister of the Veterans Administration Research Hospital in Palo Alto, California. Jones has characterized the adolescent marihuana smoker as follows:

1)—He has shifted from a self-activating, interesting and interested person to one who is withdrawn and given to disordered thinking. I have observed some degree of change of this kind in every marijuana user. . . . It is more than just a shift to sedation; thinking is affected in many ways.

2)—Thought formation in the marijuana user tends to be less powerful: conclusions are relatively impetuous, and expressed ideas are often *non sequiturs.* It is as though some of the reference checking in thinking has gone astray. The user has the illusion that his chronic state is simply a mature mellowing.

3)—The marijuana user's attention span and ability to concentrate have been reduced. Memory, especially short-term memory, is shortened.

4)—The marijuana user does not want to be "hassled." Mild criticism or merely requesting that housekeeping chores be done may be interpreted as hassling. The conflict causes the marijuana user to feel actual pain. He may even threaten his parents or other adults opposing his life style.

5)—Marijuana is a hypnotic drug, and the hypnotic spell is long lasting. Thus, the user is likely to be talked into many situations that he would otherwise avoid. He may even engage in work in which there is a follow-the-leader type of spirit. The leader, in this case, is not likely to be outside the circle of persons using marijuana. The hypnotic effects of marijuana are, in my opinion, largely responsible for the acceptance of the hazardous consequences of more powerful drugs and overly generous compliance with unreasonable requests by friends.

6)—He is likely to have a tendency toward paranoia or schizophrenia, or both. This may be caused by chronic disturbance of the neural mechanisms by which sensations received through two or more organs are synthesized into a composite interpretation of the physical cause. Such a disturbance, which occurs in both psychotic persons and those using marijuana, can lead to completely inaccurate interpretations of the real world.[47]

Hollister found that cannabis impairs short-term memory and the ability to complete thoughts during conversations.[39]

Another clinician who has been in a unique position to observe the effects of marihuana is Dr. D. Harvey Powelson, whose findings strongly substantiate those of Kolansky and Moore. Powelson was chief of the Department of Psychiatry in the Student Health Service at the University of California in Berkeley in 1965, the first year of the student riots and also the first year that marihuana and other hallucinogens were becoming widely used on college and university campuses across the country. Between 1965 and 1972, his psychiatric clinic saw between 2000 and 3000 students a year, approximately 150 to 200 of whom were sufficiently ill mentally to be hospitalized. Powelson himself personally interviewed 200 students a year, some for a single hour, others as much as two or three times a week for varying lengths of time up to five years. The remaining students were examined by clinicans under his direct supervision.

While Powelson had initially taken the stand that marihuana is a harmless drug, he was compelled by his findings to reverse his views. The first important shift in his thinking occurred as a result of observations made during psychotherapy with a young man, S., who was "bright enough to be getting his law degree and Ph.D. simultaneously and competent enough to be learning to fly and deal in real estate at the same time."[87] During the course of extended observations, Powelson came to know how S. thought—how he used or misused logic, whether or not he exercised good judgment, how well and accurately his memory worked. And in the course of therapy, Powelson began to recognize symptoms attributable to cannabis use:

> Periodically, we had hours (I was seeing him twice weekly) when his thinking became mushy. If I tried to follow him, my head began to spin. When I protested that he'd become impossible to listen to, he'd argue that his own experience was that he was thinking more clearly, more insightfully, than ever. On one such occasion, he mentioned that he'd been to a party two nights before where he'd had particularly good "grass." In Berkeley, 1968, that was not a particularly memorable remark, but we thought there might be some connection with his thinking. This same series of events recurred often enough so that I finally was able at times to post dict that S. had had some "mind-expanding drug," usually marihuana. . . .[87]

Like Kolansky and Moore, Powelson found that cannabis exacerbated the pathological aspects of thinking. Paranoia, for instance, was central to S.'s difficulties. Thus, when S. had indulged in marihuana, he became more mistrustful of Powelson and was forever "talking about his search for something or someone he could trust."[87] Simultaneously, he became adept at fooling himself about his own mental changes. When his thinking was particularly confused, he claimed that he had attained clarity and insight; when he evidenced suspicion and distrust, he maintained how "loving" and "in touch" he was.

As Powelson became familiar with the effects of cannabis on S., he learned to detect its more subtle symptoms. He also came to observe similar symptoms in numerous other individuals. The essence of the pattern he noted was that small amounts of marihuana (approximately three "joints" of street grade) interfered with memory and a sense of time. Regular use of marihuana caused increased distortions in thinking—"the user's field of interest gets narrower and narrower as he focuses his attention on immediate sensation."[87] As he consumes more of the drug, his ability to think sequentially diminishes; he becomes inadequate in areas where "judgment, memory and logic are necessary."[87] As this occurs, he develops pathological patterns of thinking. "Ultimately, all heavy users (i.e. daily users) develop a 'paranoid' way of thinking."[87]

Like Kolansky and Moore, Powelson points to the possibility that cannabis may cause permanent damage to the user:

> A frequent story is that the young person has become aware that the life he's been leading is unsatisfactory and unproductive. He then stops drugs for six months or so and reenters the university. When he returns to school, however, he finds that he can't think clearly and that, in ways he finds difficult to describe, he can't use his mind in the way he did before. Such people also seem to be aware that they've lost their will someplace, that to do something, to do anything, requires a gigantic effort—in short, they have become will-less—what we call anomic.[87]

He cites the case of a patient who was a junior faculty member at Berkeley. After dropping out, he used cannabis exclusively for 18 months in daily doses. When he realized that the drug was affecting his physical coordination, he stopped taking it and two years later returned to the University to work.

> He told me that he could no longer handle mathematics at his prior level. He simply couldn't follow the arguments anymore. Today, three and a half years later, he still cannot. He is convinced that the change is permanent and was drug-induced.[88]

Dr. Louis J. West of the Department of Psychiatry, Neurology and Behavioral Sciences at the University of Oklahoma Medical Center, has observed the same kind of individual stagnation in cannabis users that has been described by other clinicians; he, too, suggests that it may be due to a "biochemical scarring of the brain."[112]

There are many young people, including some of the brightest, who have been using marihuana now more or less regularly for three to four years. Addiction or even habituation is denied. The smoking is said to be simply for pleasure. Untoward effects are usually (not always) denied. But the experienced clinician observes in many of these individuals personality changes that may grow subtly over long periods of time: diminished drive, lessened ambition, decreased motivation, apathy, shortened attention span, distractibility, poor judgment, impaired communication skills, less effectiveness, magical thinking, derealization, depersonalization, diminished capacity to carry out complex plans or prepare realistically for the future, a peculiar fragmentation in the flow of thought, habit deterioration and progressive loss of insight. There is a clinical impression of organicity to this syndrome that I simply cannot explain away. There are too many instances of youngsters who should be getting their Ph.D.'s by now who are drifting along smoking marihuana and gradually developing these symptoms. Some of them at least are not schizophrenic, not psychopathic, not avitaminotic, not using other drugs, not simply "dropping out" by choice. And a few of the brightest ones will even tell you, "I can't even read a book from cover to cover and grasp its meaning anymore. I tell myself that I really don't care what's in it; that their topics are not important. But I really can't do it. Of course, I really don't care."[112]

These symptoms have come to be known as the "amotivational syndrome," a clinical picture described by Bejerot as "a massive and chronic passivity brought about by prolonged and intensive use of cannabis."[3]

Many other clinicians, including the Canadian psychiatrists Dr. Andrew Malcolm[64] and Dr. Conrad J. Schwarz,[96] Dr. Philip Zeidenberg of Columbia University,[116] Dr. Roy H. Hart,[31] and Dr. D.J. Spencer[101] have reported similar adverse effects on the human mind. There exists, nevertheless, a question as to whether or not moderate use of the drug poses a significant threat. Indeed, moderate use of cannabis is often equated with occasional use of alcohol. Dr. Franz E. Winkler, a private practitioner and author of one of the first articles pointing to marihuana's hazards, addresses this question:

> The lasting effects of moderate amounts of alcohol are minimal in contrast to the harmful effects of even a couple of reefers a week. . . . An early effect of marijuana and hashish use is a progressive loss of will power, already noticeable to the trained observer after about six weeks of moderate use. This loss of will power weakens the ability to resist coercion, so that marijuana users too often fall victim to hard drug pushers, extortionists and deviates. Soon all ability for real joy disappears, to be replaced by the noisy pretense of fun. While healthy teenagers will eagerly participate in all kinds of activities, such as sports, hiking, artistic endeavors, etc., a marijuana user will show an increasing tendency to talk aimlessly of great goals, while doing nothing about them.[114]

His observations are remarkably consistent with the careful accounts of practicing clinicians who have repeatedly drawn attention to evidence of personality change after fairly short periods of cannabis use. To be sure, the accounts of Kolansky and Moore, Powelson, West and others deal with obvious and in some cases extreme aberrations following rather intense or prolonged use of cannabis, but a recurring theme in many of the clinical accounts is that subtle evidence of personality disintegration from moderate use is evident to a trained observer long before the more advanced symptoms have appeared.

It should be noted that other studies on indigenous laborers in Costa Rica,[12] Jamaica[93] and Greece[18] have purported to show that even long-term use of cannabis has no significant effect on various behavioral and intellectual functions. In the Jamaica study, already referred to earlier in this article, no evidence was seen of any intellectual impairment or motivational deficit; indeed, the Jamaican laborers claimed to use high doses of cannabis as a stimulant to provide energy for strenuous physical work. In actual fact, however, the Jamaican field workers, after smoking ganja, produced less work — digging, hoeing and weeding — but executed more physical movements in doing so. The investigators somehow concluded that there was no effect of cannabis on motivation, and Zinberg and Brecher actually refer to this as evidence for a "motivational syndrome" — an enhancing effect of cannabis on motivation!

In commenting on the validity of these studies, Dr. Andrew Malcolm has written the following:

> In all of these studies, the findings have been derived from observations of a very small number of carefully selected healthy subjects; 30 in Jamaica, 41 in Costa Rica, and 47 in Greece. Most importantly, all of these 118 or so subjects were laborers or farmers who according to Soueif's findings, would be unlikely to show any appreciable changes in thinking, feeling, or acting on the basis of long-term exposure to cannabis. Commenting on these studies, Robert L. DuPont, director of the National Institute of Drug Abuse (NIDA) in the United States, said, "I think there has been a problem of overinterpreting these initial studies as showing that there are no serious health problems associated with marihuana use. This is unfortunate."[64]

The findings of Dr. M.I. Soueif of the University of Cairo, referred to by Malcolm, concern an extensive and very thorough investigation of several hundred chronic cannabis users versus a large control group in Egypt. Soueif's findings strongly suggest that the impairment of intellectual and psychomotor functions associated with chronic cannabis use varies according "to the general level of predrug proficiency. The higher the initial level of proficiency, the bigger the amount of impairment."[100] As Soueif testified to the Senate Subcommittee in 1974: "Those with a higher level of education — and/or intelligence — show the largest amount of deterioration, illiterates almost no deterioration, and semiliterates in between."[102] And other investigators have argued that many of the "findings from outside North America may not be relevant to this society. Fundamental differences in potency, form, and mode of administration of cannabis exist, and the user populations bear little resemblance to one another. . . . The user in the United States is usually under 30 years of age and is found among the most achievement-oriented social classes, in contrast to users in foreign countries, who come from the lowest, least productive strata and are well over 30."[52] And in this context one must recall the statement quoted earlier of Dr. Henry Brill regarding the cannabis experience in Jamaica, that "among the *middle class* it is now found to be associated with school dropouts, transient psychoses, panic states, and adolescent disorders. In general the effects of the drug continue to be noted as subtle and insidious."[7]

Finally, it is germane to call attention to a vast body of clinical literature on cannabis from other parts of the world over the last 50 or 100 years. In his excellent article, "A Psychiatric Classification of Cannabis Intoxication," Dr. Roy H. Hart, a practicing psychiatrist and editor of a psychiatric journal, lists an extensive bibliography of publications from the world literature concerning harmful effects of cannabis on the human psyche.[31] According to Hart, a "persistent organic brain syndrome" characterized by a)—impairment of orientation, b)—memory impairment, c)—impairment of intellectual function, d)—impaired judgment, and e)—labile and shallow affect, has long been known to be a major consequence of cannabis use in India and North Africa, but is less well known in the United States where the marihuana experience is only a decade or two old. Additional references and commentary on the world cannabis literature can be found in the various books by Nahas.[77, 80]

In summary, it is clear that a substantial body of psychiatric opinion in this country holds the view that cannabis is an extremely dangerous substance with many serious effects on the human psyche. In the past few years, it has been shown that cannabis has a direct affinity for the brain, giving weight to the hypothesis of organic damage formulated by West, Kolansky and Moore, Powelson, and others. The following section will deal with the biochemical effects of cannabis on this organ.

4. The Brain

There is no doubt that cannabis has a number of short-term effects on the brain — it could not be psychoactive if it did not. The consequences of these short-term effects are as yet uncertain; however, there is significant evidence that continuation over a period of time can produce damage to the tissues of the brain, possibly of a permanent nature.

According to Dr. W. D. M. Paton, Professor of Pharmacology at Oxford University, the various cannabinoid substances are highly soluble in fat, but have a low solubility in water.[84] Because of this fat solubility, which is exceeded only by substances such as DDT, cannabinoids can be expected to persist in the human body for a considerable period of time, and to accumulate with repeated exposure. In addition, the fat solubility makes it likely that the substances build up in nervous tissue, with its relatively high content of fatty materials.

Experimental findings have supported these contentions. The intravenous injection of radioactive delta-9-THC into laboratory rats, for example, has shown that the substance concentrates primarily in body fat, but also in the liver, lungs, reproductive organs and in the brain. THC was detected in these animals two weeks after a single injection.[57, 84] Cannabinoids are not "washed out" of the body shortly after consumption as are alcohol and its metabolic by-products, for example. An individual smoking even one marihuana cigarette a week is never free of the drug.

There is little experimental evidence dealing with the actual concentrations of THC in various organs of the human body, but there is reason to believe, based on knowledge of DDT accumulation, that the concentrations may attain high levels.

Experiments with animals have demonstrated that the toxicity of delta-9-THC also tends to be cumulative. Thus, if it is administered in very small doses, the total amount of THC needed to kill a mouse is only one-tenth of what would be needed in a single dose.[84] Cannabis is unique among drugs such as LSD and the opiates for its cumulative action.

Related to its toxicity and its tendency to accumulate in the brain is a growing body of evidence that regular marihuana use results in persistent brain damage. Dr. Robert G. Heath, Chairman of the Department of Psychiatry and Neurology at Tulane University Medical School, studied the effects of cannabis inhalation on electroencephalographic (EEG) patterns in rhesus monkeys. Heath demonstrated with objective measurements of brain wave patterns that the intake of less than two marihuana cigarettes a week for three months (a total of only 20 marihuana cigarettes!) caused serious, and quite possibly permanent, alteration of brain function in these experimental animals.[34]

In these tests, one group of animals was made to inhale cannabis smoke three times daily, five times a week, for six months (heavy dosage level); a second group inhaled somewhat less than two marihuana cigarettes a week for six months (moderate dosage); a third group received daily intravenous injections of delta-9-THC for six months. Control animals received cannabis smoke devoid of THC. Brain wave patterns were monitored regularly during the six-months test period.

According to the testimony given by Heath at the Senate Subcommittee Hearings,

> 1) — I am reporting to you that the smoke of active marihuana induced in rhesus monkeys consistent and distinct changes in [brain-wave] recordings from specific deep brain sites in association with behavioral alterations.*
> 2) — You can see under the acute effects of marihuana smoke changes in many sites. The amygdala, septal region and hippocampus show the most pronounced changes and these are brain areas where activity has been correlated with various specific emotional states. The septal region is the site for pleasure — stimulating it activates pleasure feelings. When its activity is impaired, as it is in schizophrenia, you have a lack of

*The specific "deep brain sites" referred to by Heath are located within the limbic region of the brain. The limbic region surrounds the brain stem and contains neural structures (hypothalamus, hippocampus, amygdala, septal region and others) that are directly involved in the control of the autonomic nervous system, in visceral and sexual functions, in smell and taste sensations, in the control of drives, and in the expression of emotion. The region includes the area often referred to as the "pleasure center," where electrical stimulation, both in man and animals, gives rise to highly pleasurable sensations. In one experiment using laboratory animals, tiny electrodes were implanted in specific areas of the limbic region and the animals were allowed to reward themselves with mild electrical stimulation. The animals quickly established a pattern of repetitive self-stimulation and continued until they dropped from exhaustion. Electrical stimulation of other areas in the limbic region

42

pleasure and a reduction of awareness towards a sleepy, dreamy state. The changes we found with marihuana, in some ways, resemble the changes we recorded from schizophrenics. 3)—When the monkeys were regularly exposed to these drugs, at both moderate and heavy dose levels, persistent—perhaps irreversible—alterations developed in brain function at specific deep sites where recording activity has been correlated with emotional responsivity, altering and sensory perception.[34]

Heath's testimony explicitly states that monkeys exposed to less than two marihuana cigarettes per week "began to show irreversible alteration in brain function about 3 months after onset of the experiment."[34] In describing the persistent brain wave alterations, Heath commented as follows:

It was interesting to us that these distinct and persistent brain alterations were temporarily corrected, being replaced by a different type of altered brain activity, when the animals were again exposed to the marihuana smoke. This phenomenon suggested that the marihuana had induced permanent changes of a type that could be temporarily alleviated by acute exposure, seemingly paralleling the well-known pattern of a drug-dependent person who gains temporary relief from deprivation by taking more of the drug.[34]

In these studies, Heath monitored brain-wave patterns using detecting electrodes imbedded deeply in various regions of the brain. Highly abnormal patterns were seen in several deeper regions. However, surface (scalp) electrodes applied to monkeys receiving even the high dosage levels of cannabis smoke did not show *any* abnormalities. As Heath testified, "I again cite the

---

causes pain, displeasure, fear, defensive postures and escape reactions.[48]

The limbic region is particularly sensitive to psychoactive drugs such as marihuana. Heath's studies on brain wave patterns of human patients with deeply implanted electrodes show clearly that marihuana has a direct chemical effect on the human pleasure center.[32] The immediate effects of smoking marihuana are pleasurable emotional responses and the simultaneous production of brain waves centered in the limbic region of the brain. Because of the obvious constraints on the use of human subjects, Heath has continued his work with the rhesus monkey, an animal species whose limbic region shows many parallels and similarities to man's. As described within the text of this article, chronic exposure of monkeys to cannabis smoke induces lasting EEG changes and various cellular pathological alterations within the limbic region as seen with the electron microscope.

impotence of physiological techniques of only scalp recordings used routinely on human subjects. That is the reason, of course, that people report often that there are no changes in brain functions. They use a scalp EEG, a technique which is unable to pick up these changes."[34]

In his report to the Senate Subcommittee, Heath commented on the differences between marihuana and alcohol as follows:

> Alcohol does not get in and directly affect brain function as the cannabis preparations do. They have a strikingly different physiological effect on the brain. Of course, alcohol does affect the liver and it has been shown objectively with many recent experiments that it ultimately can affect the brain, but you can use alcohol for a long period of time without producing any sort of persistent damage. People might drink rather heavily for 25 to 30 years and never get into serious trouble so far as alterations in the brain are concerned. But with marihuana, it seems as though you have to use it only for a relatively short time in moderate to heavy use before persistent behavior effects along with other evidence of brain damage begin to develop.... As data accumulate, they are beginning to confirm what many of us have suspected from clinical experience with marihuana users; namely that [marihuana] produces distinctive and irreversible changes in the brain.[34]

Heath's findings were challenged before the Senate Subcommittee by Dr. Julius Axelrod, 1970 Nobel Prize winner in neurophysiology, who felt that their significance was beclouded by what he considered were the enormous overdoses of marihuana that Heath administered to his monkeys: ". . . the doses he has given for the acute effect, for example, would be equivalent to smoking 100 marijuana cigarettes. . . . And the amount he has given for the chronic effect represents smoking 30 marijuana cigarettes three times a day for a period of six months."[1]

Even Nobel laureates occasionally are mistaken, and this was one such occasion, as Heath demonstrated by supplying the Subcommittee with the data from his experiments. The actual dosage level of heavily-dosed monkeys was 53.7 mg. delta-9-THC per month per kilogram of body weight of the monkeys. This value, although high, is still less than the 80-160 mg. of delta-9-THC per month per kilogram of body weight ingested by many of the hashish users studied in West Germany by Dr. Forrest S. Tennant and described later in this article. Moderately-dosed monkeys received 5.5 mg. delta-9-THC per month per kilogram of body weight, a level that corresponds to human consumption of about one marihuana cigarette per day.[35]

What is of interest about this exchange is that Brecher, in his *Consumer Reports* article, and Zinberg, in *Psychology Today*, both quote Axelrod at length to discredit Heath's findings. However, these same authors choose to remain silent about Heath's rebuttal, even though reference to it is made on the same page of the Hearings' transcript as the Axelrod statement which they quote.[35] Of special importance in this connection is Heath's very recent finding, as reported to an international Symposium on Marihuana held at Reims, France in July, 1978, that the blood serum levels of THC in rhesus monkeys exposed to cannabis smoke were exactly equal to serum levels of human subjects after smoking *one* marihuana joint.[36] This single finding lays to rest Axelrod's criticism beyond a shadow of a doubt.

At the same conference Heath documented, using the electron microscope, detailed structural changes at the cellular level in the brains of his experimental monkeys.[36] These alterations included a)—widening of the synaptic cleft (juncture between adjacent nerve cells), b)—abnormal deposits of dense material in the region of the synaptic cleft, c)—clumping of synaptic vesicles—an early sign of nerve cell degeneration,[30] and d)—fragmentation and disorientation of the rough endoplasmic reticulum (structures within the cell involved in protein synthesis).[76] All of these changes were localized within the septal region of the limbic area, where Heath previously had recorded persistent, abnormal brain wave patterns.

It will be exceedingly difficult to repeat Heath's monkey experiments with human subjects, but it is abundantly clear that his findings lend very strong support to the hypothesis that marihuana causes organic damage to the tissues of the brain. As such, they stand as powerful and enduring testimony to the dangers of marihuana use.

Other types of evidence have accumulated concerning the effects of marihuana on the brain. Dr. Peter A. Fried of Carleton University, Ottawa, has found that young rats subjected to cannabis smoke not only suffered from generally reduced body weight, but also had significantly smaller hearts and brains as a percentage of their total body weight.[2] The fact that Fried got approximately similar results with young suckling rats whose mothers were exposed to marihuana smoke strongly suggests the transmission of marihuana products, quite possibly THC, through the mother's milk to the offspring.[21] Dr. Harold Kalant of the Department of Pharmacology at the University of Toronto has found that rats exposed to marihuana smoke for five months' time suffered an irreversible loss of learning ability as measured by standard psychological tests.[17]

In a preliminary study conducted in 1971, the late Dr. A.M.G. Campbell of the Royal United Hospital, Bristol, England, reported that chronic marihuana smokers aged 18 to 26 had suffered as much brain atrophy as is normally encountered in very elderly people.[8] Campbell and colleagues performed air encephalography, a type of X-ray procedure in which air is injected into the cavities of the brain, on ten young men who had used cannabis consistently over a period of 3 to 11 years. Each of the ten subjects displayed severe personality changes, including memory loss of recent events, hallucinations, a reversal of sleep rhythms, and other mental effects. Comparison with air encephalograms of carefully matched control subjects indicated that certain brain tissue of the cannabis users had physically atrophied. Since none of the patients displayed clear evidence of any conditions prior to cannabis use that might cause degeneration of brain tissue, Campbell concluded that "regular use of cannabis produces cerebral atrophy in young adults."[8] Some investigators have taken issue with Campbell's conclusions,[55] because several of the ten subjects had used amphetamines and/or LSD in addition to cannabis. Campbell emphasized, however, that although other substances had been taken, cannabis was the predominant drug in all cases.

More recently, two groups of medical investigators have measured ventricular size in the brains of chronic marihuana smokers using computerized axial tomography (CAT scan), a complex X-ray procedure, and have failed to confirm Campbell's finding of cerebral atrophy.[11, 58] The discrepancy between these findings and those of Campbell can be resolved only by further study. In this regard, however, Dr. Hardin B. Jones claims to have applied appropriate statistical methods to the newer data and shown that there were indeed significant differences in ventricular sizes between cannabis users and control subjects.[49] It is to be hoped that Jones' analysis will be published and subjected to the scrutiny of peer review.

There are too few reliable data presently available to permit a valid conclusion concerning marihuana use and cerebral atrophy, but the seriousness of such an effect, if it exists, should make it an important priority for further neurological study.

5. The Lungs

Recent clinical evidence and findings from several research laboratories demonstrate that cannabis inhalation has severely damaging effects on human lung tissue. Testimony on this subject before the Senate Subcommittee on Internal Security was summarized in two major conclusions:

> 1)—Chronic cannabis smoking can produce sinusitis, pharyngitis, bronchitis, emphysema and other respiratory difficulties in a year or less, as opposed to ten or twenty years of cigarette smoking to produce similar complications.
> 2)—Cannabis smoke, or cannabis smoke mixed with [tobacco] cigarette smoke, is far more damaging to lung tissue than tobacco smoke alone.[66]

The damage is described as "pre-cancerous."

Much of the evidence in support of these contentions comes from the extensive observations of Dr. Forrest S. Tennant, Jr., who headed the U.S. Army's drug program in Europe from 1968 to 1972. Tennant conducted detailed studies on the relation between the high incidence of severe respiratory problems in American soldiers and the use of the potent hashish preparations available to these men.[108] Of particular note was the appearance of what Tennant termed "hashish bronchitis"[107] and emphysema. As Paton testified in the Senate Hearings, "Emphysema is normally a disease of much later life; but now the quite unexpected prospect of a new crop of respiratory cripples early in life is opening up."[84] Tennant observed, "Even though a person can get bronchitis and emphysema from cigarette smoking, one must usually smoke cigarettes for 10-20 years to get these complications. We became alarmed about this because we began seeing these conditions in 18-, 19-, and 20-year-old men."[108] The cellular lesions found in bronchial biopsies of these men were identified as *squamous cell metaplasia,* a condition well known to be "statistically and anatomically linked with carcinoma of the lung."[107]

The subjects in Tennant's study absorbed very heavy doses of hashish smoke, and the results are not directly applicable to more moderate cannabis users. However, the alarming rapidity with which severe respiratory problems developed, coupled with the cumulative nature of cannabis action, raises the very real possibility of serious pulmonary disease in moderate smokers who use cannabis over a longer period of time. Indeed, clinical data from at least two other researchers show that moderate to heavy smoking "may induce clinically significant changes in pulmonary function."[69, 106] These changes are said to be "rather insidious and not easily detectable by routine health examination."[69]

The caustic and irritating effects of cannabis smoke are well known to all users, and recent work has shown that "like tar from tobacco cigarettes, reefer tar is carcinogenic when painted onto mouse skin."[84] Paton has stated the following:

> Cannabis has not been used extensively in a society with an expectation of life long enough to show a carcinogenic effect, until recent years. In effect, a new experiment in cancer epidemiology started 5 to 10 years ago.... I believe that medical epidemiological studies of the pulmonary pathology of cannabis are now urgent for getting an early warning of a carcinogenic situation.[84]

The careful investigations of Dr. Harris Rosenkrantz of the Mason Research Institute in Worcester, Massachusetts have shown that chronic exposure of laboratory rats to cannabis smoke produces serious alteration of lung tissue including a) — an intensive inflammatory response, b) — the breakdown of air sacs in the lung, and c) — the formation of "cholesterol clefts" in the lung tissue.[92] In these studies marihuana smoke was delivered from a specially constructed inhalation device and the doses were carefully adjusted to correspond to levels of human consumption. Control experiments clearly demonstrated that marihuana effects were far more deleterious than equivalent exposure to tobacco smoke.

Additional supporting evidence showing lung damage has come from the laboratory studies of Dr. Cecile Leuchtenberger of the Swiss Institute for Experimental Cancer Research, Lausanne.[59, 60, 61] Working with small portions of excised mouse lung tissue cultured in a suitable nutrient fluid, Leuchtenberger showed that daily exposure to standardized puffs of marihuana smoke over a period of five consecutive days significantly altered the morphological appearance of these cells, interfered with cell division, and affected both the content and synthesis of DNA, the all-important genetic material of the cell.[61] The cellular changes noted were described as "pre-cancerous"; tobacco smoke had a much smaller effect. Similar studies with portions of living human lung tissue gave comparable results.[59]

Leuchtenberger has also undertaken a study of the effects of standaridized doses of cannabis on respiratory processes in laboratory mice. Preliminary results indicate an effect from low doses of cannabis smoke on terminal bronchioles in these animals.[60] In summarizing her work Leuchtenberger states:

> The observations that marihuana cigarette smoke stimulates irregular growth in the respiratory system which resembles closely precancerous lesions would indicate that long-term inhalation of marihuana cigarette smoke may either directly evoke lung cancer or may at least contribute to the development of lung cancer.... Consequently, further extensive research is urgently needed to explore chronic effects of marihuana smoke on cells and tissues.[59]

6. The Immune System

A great deal of recent medical research has centered on the effects of marihuana on the immune system, that is, the capacity of the body to resist infectious agents and other foreign elements such as tissue transplants and cancer cells. Although the results of this research are not yet conclusive, there is strong evidence to suggest that THC suppresses the immune system of rodents and other experimental animals, and several reports pointing to this possibility in man.

One of the first studies concerning the effects of marihuana on the immune system in man was conducted by Dr. Gabriel G. Nahas, Research Professor of Anesthesiology at the College of Physicians and Surgeons, Columbia University. Nahas and his associates tested certain aspects of the immune response of 51 marihuana smokers, 16 to 35 years of age, who had smoked an average of four marihuana cigarettes a week for at least one year.[78] Lymphocytes, a class of white blood cells found in the body and known to play a key role in the body's defense system, were removed from these subjects and stimulated to undergo cell division. (Lymphocytes are cells that ordinarily divide very rapidly when the body is attacked by a virus or foreign tissue.) The rate of division of these cells was measured and found to be 41% lower in the cannabis smokers than in a control group of cells from non-smokers. A comparable diminution of this response was noted in 60 cancer patients, 26 uremic patients, and in 24 kidney transplant patients who were receiving immunosuppressive drugs to prevent rejection of their transplanted organs.

In subsequent investigations Nahas demonstrated that normal lymphocytes from the blood of non-marihuana smokers, when cultured in nutrient fluid in the presence of THC, cannabadiol (CBD), or cannabinol (CBN), were seriously impaired in their capacity to undergo cellular division.[79, 80, 82] This important result provides a convincing demonstration of THC effects at the cellular level. Indeed, the finding that THC and various other cannabinoid substances strongly inhibit cellular processes was fully documented by no less than 12 medical research groups at an international conference on marihuana held in Helsinki in the summer of 1975.[81] These researchers reported that cannabis substances strongly interfere with the synthesis of DNA, RNA and protein in a wide variety of cell types, including a selection of human cell lines; that cell division and the rate of tissue growth are impaired; and that cells treated with cannabinoids undergo abnormal division, producing aberrant nuclei with subnormal amounts of DNA. As stated by Dr. W.D.M. Paton, one of the organizers of the conference, there appear to be at least two target organs for cannabis, apart from the brain, in which the cellular effects are prominent, (1) the testis and (2) the immune system.

The effect of marihuana on the immune system has been described by a number of researchers: Cushman and co-workers reported impairment of T-lymphocytes in chronic marihuana smokers;[26] Petersen and Lemberger described impairment of lymphocyte activity in cannabis users and showed in addition that polymorphonuclear phagocytes, a type of white blood cell that engulfs foreign substances, were also seriously reduced in number;[86] Harris and colleague demonstrated that delta-9-THC delays the rejection of skin grafts in laboratory mice by as much as 42 percent;[62] Rosenkrantz described strong immunosuppressive effects in rodents;[89] Stefanis and Issidorides gave evidence of white blood cell changes in chronic hashish smokers in Greece;[102] Chari-Bitron showed that THC leads to paralysis of alveolar macrophages, cells considered to be the first line of defense in the human lung.[9] Several other investigators have been unable to detect an effect of THC on the immune system of man,[97, 113] and further research work will be needed to resolve the disparity between these findings and those cited above.

The medical implications of this work are very serious indeed. There is growing evidence to suggest that lymphocytes play a significant role in the body's resistance to cancer. Recent research supports the idea that numerous cancer cells arise within the body every day, but the healthy human organism has the capacity to resist and destroy them. Indeed, according to a recent statistical study, kidney transplant patients given immunosuppressive drugs to prevent organ rejection develop cancer at rates 80 times that of the general population.[85] Any impairment of the system of defense mechanisms and immune responses, therefore, carries with it the distinct risk of malignancy and other serious pathological conditions. Long-term epidemiological studies will be needed to identify the actual connection between marihuana use and disease.

7. Reproductive Processes

Clinical observations, laboratory studies with human subjects and numerous animal experiments all point to serious effects of marihuana on processes of reproduction. Dr. Robert C. Kolodny of the Reproductive Biology Research Foundation in St. Louis states that cannabis may cause "disruption of sperm production, the possibility of birth defects, the possibility of impairment of hormone balance and the possibility of either inhibition of puberty or disruption of normal sexual differentiation during fetal development."[55]

Working with Drs. William H. Masters and Gelson Toro of the Reproductive Biology Research Foundation, Kolodny studied a group of 20 young men, 18 to 28 years of age, who had used cannabis for at least six months, for an average of 9.4 times per week.[55] None of these subjects had ever used LSD or other hallucinogenic drugs, had any history of hormone imbalance, or showed evidence of prior liver disease. Twenty similarly screened individuals served as controls. The important finding was that testosterone,* the principal male hormone, was reduced in amount by 44% in the cannabis users. Subjects who had smoked more than ten times per week had lower levels of testosterone than those using cannabis less than ten times per week.

Six out of 17 individuals tested showed highly reduced sperm counts; two were found to be clinically sterile.

Kolodny's findings have seemingly been contradicted by a later study conducted by Dr. Jack H. Mendelson and associates at the Alcohol and Drug Abuse Research Center, Harvard Medical School-McLean Hospital. During 21 days of progressively increasing marihuana consumption under controlled hospital conditions, Mendelson's group found no decrease in testosterone level in any of their 27 young male subjects.[68] This result was cited by Brecher to bolster his case for the *Consumer Reports* article.[6] In point of fact, however, no conflict exists between Mendelson's

---

*Testosterone, a steroid hormone produced by the testes, plays an important role in primary sexual differentiation during embryonic development, in secondary sexual changes occurring during adolescence, and in the production of functional sperm by the adult male.

results and those of Kolodny. Kolodny, in tests at the University of California at Los Angeles, confirmed Mendelson's finding that there is no decrease in testosterone level during the first three weeks of marihuana use. He did, however, observe a marked decrease beginning around the fifth week.[56]

There are other ways in which marihuana is suspected of affecting the reproductive processes. Hall's experience of 20% incidence of sexual impotence among long-term ganja smokers in Jamaica has already been cited,[28] and similar reports are known from private physicians in Morocco and India, where cannabis is widely used, as well as in the United States.[48] Kolodny also has observed instances of impotence in several of his subjects. Discontinuing marihuana use led to normal sexual functioning in every case.[55]

Several very serious implications arise from these studies. First, from animal experiments it is known that several cannabis constituents pass across the placental barrier into the developing fetus. Normal sexual development in males takes place during the fourth month of embryonic life and is dependent upon adequate levels of testosterone. Interference with testosterone production at this critical time could seriously impair primary sexual differentiation in unborn male children.

Secondly, marihuana products could seriously damage normal processes of sexual maturation in teenage boys undergoing adolescence. The increasing use of cannabis in the lower high school grades and in the junior high school years renders this an alarming possibility.

Thirdly, the diminished testosterone content and the possible connection between sexual impotence and cannabis use jeopardizes the ability of an adult male cannabis user to experience normal sexual functioning.

Recent medical research has added another finding to the list of cannabis effects on the human male. Dr. John W. Harmon of New England Deaconess Hospital, Brookline, Massachusetts and Dr. Menalaos A. Aliapoulios, Associate Professor of Surgery at Harvard Medical School, described the apparent connection between cannabis use and gynecomastia, a feminizing change in men in which there is considerable enlargement of the breasts.[29] These researchers now know of 16 patients with marihuana-related gynecomastia. Four have requested surgical removal of the breast tissue; three have reported a reduction in breast size and a decrease in touch sensitivity following abstinence from marihuana. This effect of cannabis is restricted to a small percentage of marihuana users, possibly those with an unusual hormone balance, but it is nevertheless a clearly demonstrated result and should not be discounted because of its relative infrequency.

A recent study on spayed female rats injected with THC has shown that THC acts like the female sex hormone estrogen in a standard test for estrogen activity.[98] This finding gives considerable support to the idea that many of the effects of marihuana on human males—depressed testosterone levels, gynecomastia, reduced sperm counts—can be explained by the estrogen-like effects of THC, for it is well-known that female hormone produces these same physiological effects in male human beings.

Another area of active investigation centers on the connection between cannabis use and birth defects.* During the past 10 years several research groups have studied possible teratogenic effects of marihuana in various animal species, especially rodents. Because of conflicting reports in the literature, a comprehensive study was undertaken in the early 1970s by the U.S. National Institute of Drug Abuse (N.I.D.A.) and this study concluded that delta-9-THC does not seem to exert a serious teratogenic effect on rodent embryos at behaviorally effective dose levels.[27] In a recent review of the literature, Dr. Harris Rosenkrantz of the Mason Research Institute and Dr. Monique Braude of N.I.D.A. reaffirmed this conclusion.[90] However, in an extensive series of tests, Dr. Rosenkrantz has fully documented another type of biological damage, an embryocidal (embryo killing) effect of cannabis, in several strains of laboratory rodents. As Rosenkrantz reported to the Reims conference, *"In utero* deaths occur at dosage levels comparable to human consumption."[91] The specific effects include single embryo and whole litter resorptions during development (i.e. the rodent embryos

---

*Environmental influences (usually within the womb) which cause impairment of normal embryonic development are termed *teratogenic agents*. Congenital abnormalities of this kind are not inherited conditions but result from toxicity to various tissues at crucial stages of growth and development. The best known examples of teratogens are *Rubella* (German measles virus) and the chemical substance thalidomide.

degenerate within the uterus and the tissue remains are resorbed by the mother animal). The effects occur during the first six days of pregnancy and may represent an effect of cannabis on the proper establishment of fetal circulation by which essential nutrients pass from mother to offspring. The conclusion of Dr. H. Tuchmann-Duplessis of Paris at the Reims symposium that marihuana, although not teratogenic, is embryocidal is supported by a strong foundation of research studies from many laboratories and must be considered a firm scientific result.

The findings of Dr. Peter A. Fried of the Department of Psychology, Carleton University, Ottawa agree with those of Rosenkrantz, and provide additional evidence for pre-natal effects in laboratory animals. According to Fried, "exposure to cannabinoids during fetal development ... has multiple effects on rats,"[21] including a significant decrease in birth weight, a delay in physiological development after birth, and a long-lasting sensitivity to cannabis (i.e. a significantly longer time to develop tolerance). Although Fried found no evidence of teratogenesis in his study, he did observe a substantial percentage of fetal resorptions in mother rats exposed to cannabis during the first few days of pregnancy.[21]

Another highly significant finding was that male and female offspring of pregnant rats treated with cannabis had smaller reproductive organs and were significantly less fertile. Indeed, exposure to cannabis smoke in the fetal stage had a much greater effect on fertility than injections of delta-9-THC into adult rats two months prior to mating. Finally, offspring born to these less fertile F_1 rats weighed less and were slower to develop certain reflexes. In this latter case, it is to be emphasized, the effects of cannabis seen in the F_2 generation were "a function of moderate amounts of cannabis smoke administered *two generations* earlier"[22] (emphasis added).

Dr. Ethel Sassenrath of the Primate Research Center of the University of California at Davis has maintained a large breeding colony of group-living macaques (rhesus monkeys) for six years, and together with Dr. Loring F. Chapman is studying the effects of long-term exposure to delta-9-THC on social behavior in this species. Behavioral changes best described as "increased irritable aggressiveness" have been noted in rhesus monkeys chronically treated with delta-9-THC, especially in animals simultaneously exposed to chronic social stress.[95] As summarized by these investigators in their report to the Reims conference in July, 1978:

> Prolonged chronic exposure to THC affects the quality and degree of behavioral responses to social stress (such as threats, irritants, or challenges) to produce a non-adaptive over-responsiveness, or apparent inability to cope. In group-living rhesus monkeys this state is manifest as increased "irritable aggression"... Most of the predominant behavioral effects of long-term exposure of primates appear to have counterparts in behavioral effects reported by observers of chronic marihuana use in man. This lends credence to the concept of direct neuro-pharmacological effect of the drug on brain centers controlling behavior.[95]

Most significantly, Sassenrath and Chapman have compiled extensive breeding records to show a truly alarming incidence of reproductive failures in THC-treated rhesus monkeys, at dosage levels comparable to human consumption of one or two joints per day.[94] Forty-four percent of all offspring conceived by THC-treated females resulted in spontaneous abortion, fetal death, stillbirth or death of the infant shortly after birth. (Control data for untreated female monkeys showed approximately eight percent loss of infants, mostly from pneumonia.) Detailed *post mortem* study of the offspring from the cannabis treated mothers revealed a wide variety of apparently non-specific histo-pathologies ranging from hydrocephalus (fluid accumulation in the brain), other brain alterations, vascular, liver and kidney deficiencies, and others. Apparently cannabis does not produce a highly specific birth defect syndrome (such as the well-known stunting of limb formation induced by thalidomide), but the data clearly demonstrate a high incidence of embryocidal and feticidal effects of delta-9-THC in primate species thought to metabolize marihuana very similarly to man.

Sassenrath and Chapman have not been able to pinpoint the mode of action of delta-9-THC, but they suggest that the reproductive losses may represent direct toxicity to the developing fetus, or possibly an effect on the maternal support system, i.e. the supply of nourishment from mother to offspring through the placenta. Of added concern is the finding that those viable offspring born to THC-treated mothers were below average in weight, presented higher frequencies of assorted infections and other health problems, and displayed hyperactivity and an apparent tendency toward overresponsiveness to environmental stimuli.

Because of the obvious moral and legal restraints on medical experimentation with human mothers, it will probably never be possible to prove in a rigorous scientific manner that cannabis interferes with human embryonic development. Data drawn from birth clinics in Washington, D.C. show a pronounced increase in abnormal births and reproductive failures in mothers with a history of multiple drug use (including cannabis and LSD) both before and during pregnancy,[44] but the controlled conditions through which one could demonstrate causal effects of marihuana (or LSD) use on the human fetus are obviously lacking. However, the comprehensive and meticulously executed animal studies of Rosenkrantz, together with the important findings of Fried, Sassenrath and Chapman, constitute a serious indictment of cannabis, and provide a sober warning to any prospective human mother concerning her capacity to conceive and nurture a normal, healthy child. Perhaps the greatest tragedy of all is the almost exact correspondence between the ages of most frequent drug use (late teens through late twenties) and the reproductive period during which most American women bear children.

8. The Genes and Chromosomes

One final area of study centers on the effect of marihuana derivatives on the human genetic material, the genes and chromosomes. Of particular importance is the finding that cannabis products are absorbed into the ovaries and testes. Repeated exposure probably leads to a gradual buildup in the reproductive organs.

In one of the first studies on cannabis and human chromosomes, Dr. Morton A. Stenchever tested white blood cell chromosomes of 49 cannabis users versus a control group of 20 non-users.[104] The results showed a high rate of chromosome breakage in users, an average of 3.4 breaks per 100 cells, versus 1.2 breaks per 100 cells for the controls. In addition, many abnormally appearing cells were observed in blood samples drawn from the cannabis users. Stenchever's results confirm the earlier findings of Dr. Douglas G. Gilmour of New York University who found significant chromosome breaks in 11 individuals who had used cannabis for several years.[23]

Several investigators, including Stenchever,[103] have been unable to show chromosome alterations in test tube cultures grown in the presence of delta-9-THC, and at least one study on short-term use in man has failed to disclose evidence of chromosome damage.[83] At this time, there is no conclusive evidence to show that marihuana use causes chromosome breaks in man and further work is obviously needed.

Other types of chromosome alteration have been described by Dr. Akira Morishima of the College of Physicians and Surgeons, Columbia University, who demonstrated that as many as 30 percent of the lymphocytes of chronic marihuana smokers contained a highly reduced number of chromosomes, from 5 to 30, instead of the normal complement of 46.[73, 74] He proposed that, "marihuana smoking results in severe disruption of the normal process by which chromosomes segregate into succeeding generations of cells"[73] during cell division. More recently, Morishima has demonstrated that delta-9-THC and other cannabinoids seriously alter the normal process of mitosis in test tube experiments, and produce the same marked reduction in chromosome number as he previously noted in cannabis smokers.[74, 75] Further work is needed to evaluate the

59

medical implications of these findings, but it is clear that chromosome damage of any kind poses several serious dangers to normal health. Chromosomal abnormalities in somatic cells* of the user may underlie leukemia and other forms of malignancy, as well as additional pathological conditions. Secondly, chromosome damage to the gonadal tissue of the user may seriously affect the physical and mental development of children conceived from germ cells (sperm or egg)* carrying the defective chromosomes. It is not known at this time whether cannabis derivatives actually cause chromosome damage in human gonadal tissue, but many physical and chemical agents affecting the genes and chromosomes of somatic cells also affect reproductive tissue.

Numerous reports in the medical literature describe serious effects of marihuana on reproductive cells in animals, and at least two studies cite sperm damage in man. Dr. Cecile Leuchtenberger reported that fresh smoke from marihuana cigarettes affected not only the DNA content of human and mouse lung tissue,[59, 61] but also reduced the DNA content of spermatids (immature sperm) in gonadal tissue explants of the mouse.[60] Almost 50 percent of the mouse spermatids showed reduced amounts of DNA following daily administration of two to six standardized puffs of marihuana smoke over the course of several days. Similar exposure to tobacco smoke had no effect on the mouse spermatids.

Leuchtenberger's work complements the findings of Dr. V. P. Dixit,[15] who demonstrated that the administration of relatively low doses of cannabis extracts to young adult male mice produced a complete arrest of sperm formation and a regression of Leydig cells (gonadal cells responsible for the production of male hormone). In these experiments cannabis extract produced degenerative changes both in spermatids and in mature sperm of the experimental mice. Three investigators at the Reims symposium described harmful effects of cannabis on sperm formation in rodents. Dr. Arthur Zimmerman of the University of Toronto, Dr. H. Huang of

---

*Somatic or body cells (muscle, nerve, skin, lung, blood, etc.) play no role in determining the inherited characteristics of subsequent generations. Chromosome breakage in these cells affects only the individual in whom the damage has occurred. Germ or sex cells (sperm and egg), on the other hand, are responsible for determining the inherited traits. Chromosome damage or other forms of genetic mutation in these cells is directly inherited.

Columbia University and Dr. G.I. Fujimoto of Albert Einstein Medical College found that exposure to cannabis caused a)—serious disruption of the early stages of sperm differentiation,[41, 117] b)—chromosome damage of several kinds,[117] c)—produced abnormal sperm with altered morphology,[41, 117] and d)—interfered with DNA synthesis during sperm formation.[41]

Finally, two studies have given evidence for marihuana effects on sperm formation in man. In a prospective study of 16 male cannabis smokers, Dr. Wylie C. Hembree of Columbia University showed a significant effect of cannabis on the production of human sperm.[37, 38] After one month of heavy smoking in a rigorously controlled hospital setting, the subjects showed a)—a marked reduction in sperm count, b)—decreased sperm mobility, and c)—many sperm of abnormal appearance. Drs. C. N. Stefanis and M. Issidorides cited morphological alterations in the sperm of chronic hashish users in Greece, which included the loss of essential proteinaceous substances in the sperm (see photograph on p. 67).[102] Although the precise nature of cannabis effects on sperm formation and function in man is unclear at this time, there is sufficient evidence, both from animal and human studies, to warrant grave concern over possible genetic consequences. As Stenchever has written, "The magnitude of the problem could be overwhelming when one considers the number of young people using the drug. The priority assigned to such studies should be the highest possible."[104]

9. Tolerance

It is now firmly established through carefully controlled laboratory study that a profound tolerance* develops to many of the behavioral and pharmacological effects of THC in all animal species that have been tested with the drug. Birds, rats, dogs, and various primates require much higher dosage levels within a few weeks to alter basic physiological functions or to impair learned responses in simple psychological tests. Additional observations clearly demonstrate tolerance to THC in man. These findings conclusively refute the notion of "reverse tolerance" (less drug needed to produce a given response), that has been part of the popular lore of drug use for some years.

The careful studies of D.E. McMillan and colleagues on tolerance to drug effects in pigeons clearly illustrate the nature of this phenomenon.[63] Laboratory pigeons in this study were given doses of THC (0.3-1 mg/kg body weight) to abolish a learned pecking response. After five days at this level, the birds resumed pecking. The dose was then increased 20-fold until the birds became tolerant, and gradually increased further to 180 mg/kg over a period of one month. (180 mg/kg is a lethal dose to a non-tolerant bird.) In subsequent investigations the dosage tolerated was further elevated to 1600 mg/kg, a 5300-fold increase in amount or about nine times the ordinary lethal dosage.[19] Upon cessation of drug administration, there were no obvious withdrawal symptoms, but tolerance persisted and was still observed 30 days later.

Tolerance in man, first indicated by the 1894 report of the Indian Hemp Drug Commission,[42] is supported by many clinical observations. Miras reported that "hashish smokers he has known in Greece for 20 years are able to smoke 10 times as much as other people. If a beginner smoked the same quantity he would collapse."[70] Other relevant findings have been reported by Tennant for American soldiers stationed in West Germany,[108] by Jones for subjects at the Langley-Porter Neuropsychiatric Institute in San Francisco,[50] and by Hembree and Nahas for volunteer subjects at Columbia-Presbyterian Hospital in New York.[37, 38] In the latter

*Tolerance is said to develop when increasing doses of a drug are required to produce the same effect.

62

study chronic cannabis users, confined in hospital and given marihuana cigarettes *ad libitum* under carefully monitored conditions, smoked 5 to 20 potent marihuana cigarettes a day. Consumption by these individuals (up to 360 mg THC per day) corresponds to the very high daily intake reported for chronic marihuana users in Jamaica, Costa Rica and Morocco who are tolerant to large amounts of cannabis. A similar dose in a novice would produce acute psychotomimetic toxicity.

Tolerance to cannabis provides a physiological basis for the necessity of the heavy chronic smoker to increase dosage, or to use more potent psychoactive drugs such as LSD, cocaine and heroin.[77] This does not mean that every regular marihuana smoker will necessarily move on to other more powerful drugs, but a significant portion does, quite possibly because they have become tolerant to high levels of marihuana and must seek additional stimulation from more potent substances. This notion becomes especially alarming when one notes that in 1977 there were estimated to be over four million chronic marihuana users in the United States, many of them teenagers, and the number of users in this country at all levels of consumption is escalating at a rapid rate.

10. Is Marihuana Addictive?
Physical and Psychological Dependence

One of the widely held misconceptions regarding drug use concerns the distinction between addictive and non-addictive substances. Addiction, by which is meant physical dependence accompanied by withdrawal symptoms upon abstinence, is often the significant criterion by which the harmfulness of a drug both to an individual and to society is assessed. Measured by this standard, marihuana, which is not physically addictive except at very high dosage levels and which does not produce the distress, chills, diarrhea, and pain of heroin withdrawal, is held to be a relatively safe, "recreational" drug that can be used or not, according to one's wishes. Recent advocacy of cocaine use is based upon a similar claim of non-addiction.

What is overlooked by those who focus principally on physical dependence is the more subtle but no less real psychological dependence that is so much a part of marihuana use. As Nahas has so cogently stated:

> The desire for instant gratification is a profound psychological reinforcer. Physical dependence does not develop with central nervous system stimulants such as cocaine, which is known to create in an individual one of the most enslaving types of drug dependence. Addiction to a drug is not a function of the ability of the drug to produce withdrawal symptoms. Drug dependence results basically from the reproducible interaction between an individual and a pleasure-inducing biologically active molecule. The common denominator of all drug dependence is the psychological reinforcement resulting from reward associated with past [use of the drug] and the subsequent increasing desire for repeated reinforcement.[77]

Abstinence from chronic use of marihuana produces relatively mild symptoms (at least when judged by the standard of heroin withdrawal) of irritability, insomnia and loss of appetite, but it is abundantly clear that cannabis can produce a psychological dependence that is a formidable obstacle to discontinuance of its use. The observations of D. C. M. Yardley on undergraduate students at Oxford in 1965 are typical of many such accounts of psychological dependence:

Everyone of those who were regular takers seemed to be convinced that *Cannabis* was not habit forming; that they had not developed any real habit of taking it; and that they could give up the drug at any time at will. . . . But most of those who had become accustomed to taking this drug regularly had to call on professional help to give it up. Furthermore, it was plain that those who did take it regularly tended gradually to increase their consumption and a certain number of them, small but perhaps significant, graduated to hard drugs.[115]

The American soldiers studied by Tennant in West Germany did not wish to give up hashish smoking inspite of severe impairment of their physical health from cannabis, and other studies have identified similar attitudes among cannabis users in Israel, Egypt, Greece, and elsewhere. Marihuana is not an addictive drug in the usual sense, but it must surely be considered a habit-forming substance that often produces profound psychological dependence.

11. Conclusion

While further research remains to be done, there is already a large body of hard evidence available for anyone who wishes to reach an informed opinion, or to counsel those who seek advice. When I have reviewed some of the material presented here with my own students, the reaction has been mixed. Many have been deeply impressed by the consistency of the findings and the seriousness of the observed effects. But others remain adamant in their rejection of all unfavorable testimony. Perhaps their attitude should come as no surprise, for proof of physical harm alone has never been an effective deterrent to self-indulgence.

There is, of course, another dimension altogether to the marihuana question. Inescapably, the time comes when each must ask himself: What kind of person do I want to be? What kind of society do I want to live in? To pursue the ethical and social implications of marihuana use would lead me far beyond the intended scope of this article. And yet it is on just such considerations that the decision ultimately rests. I wish therefore to leave one question with the reader: Can the use of marihuana, in *any* amount, ever be reconciled with the clarity of thought, the personal integrity and the strength of will that an individual must have who would play an active role in helping humanity find the way out of its presently severe and ever-worsening difficulties?

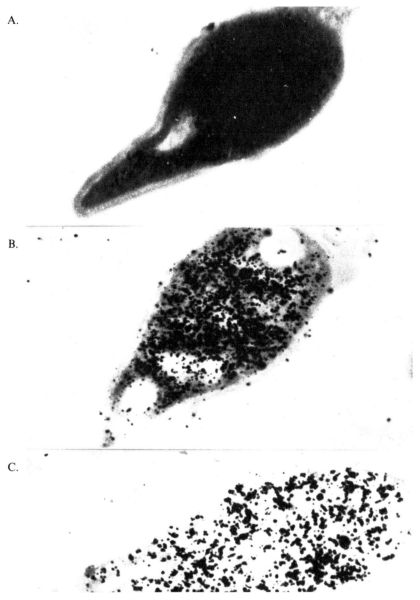

A.

B.

C.

Electron Microscope Pictures of Spermatozoa

A. Spermatozoa from a control subject.
B. and C. Spermatozoa from chronic hashish users in Athens, Greece.

Spermatozoa from hashish users show a decreased amount of essential proteinaceous substances. (From the work of Stefanis and Issidorides, 1976.[102] See p. 61)

12. References

1. Axelrod, J. (1974). Testimony before the Senate Subcommittee on Internal Security, May, 1974, ref. 66, pp. 142-146.

2. Barnes, C. and Fried, P.A. (1974). Tolerance to delta-9-THC in adult rats with differential delta-9-THC exposure when immature or during early adulthood. Psychopharmacologia *34*: 181-190.

3. Bejerot, N. (1974). Testimony before the Senate Subcommittee on Internal Security, May, 1974, ref. 66, pp. 170-177.

4. Braenden, O.J. (1972). Testimony before the Senate Subcommittee on Internal Security, Sept. 18, 1972.

5. Brecher, E.M. and Editors of Consumer Reports. (1972). *Licit and Illicit Drugs,* Consumers Union Report, Little, Brown and Co., Boston and Toronto.

6. Brecher, E.M. and Editors of Consumer Reports. (1975). Marijuana: The health questions. Consumer Reports *40:* 143-149.

7. Brill, H. (1974). Testimony before the Senate Subcommittee on Internal Security, May, 1974, ref. 66, pp. 30-36.

8. Campbell, A.M.G., Evans, M., Thompson, J.L.G. and Williams, M.J. (1971). Cerebral atrophy in young cannabis smokers. Lancet 2(7736): 1219-1224.

9. Chari-Bitron, A. (1976). Effect of delta-9-tetrahydrocannabinol on red blood cell membranes and on alveolar macrophages, ref. 81, pp. 273-282.

10. Clark, L.D. and Nakashima, E.N. (1968). Experimental studies of marihuana. Am. J. Psychiat. *125:* 135-140.

11. Co, B.T., Goodwin, D.W., Gado, M., Mikhael, M., and Hill, S.Y. (1977). Absence of cerebral atrophy in chronic cannabis users. J. Amer. Med. Assoc. *237:* 1231-1232.

12. Coggins, W.J. (1976). Costa Rica cannabis project: An interim report on the medical aspects. In: *Pharmacology of Marihuana,* Braude, M.C. and Szara, S. (eds.). Raven Press, New York, pp. 667-670.

13. Cowan, K. (1974). Testimony before the Senate Subcommittee on Internal Security, May, 1974, ref. 66, pp. 250-264.

14. Crancer, A., Jr., Dille, J.M., Delay, J.M., Wallace, J.E. and Haykin, M.D. (1969). Comparison of the effects of marihuana and alcohol on simulated driving performance. Science *164:* 851-854.

15. Dixit, V.P., Sharma, V.N., and Lohiya, N.K. (1974). The effect of chronically administered cannabis extract on the testicular function of mice. Europ. J. Pharmacol. *26:* 111-114.

16. DuPont, R.L. (1975). Testimony before the Senate Subcommittee on Internal Security, May, 1975, ref. 67, pp. 461-471.

17. Fehr, K.A., Kalant, H., LeBlanc, A.E. and Knox, G.V. (1976). Permanent learning impairment after chronic heavy exposure to cannabis or ethanol in the rat, ref. 81, pp. 495-505.

18. Fink, M., Volavka, J., Panagiotopoulos, C.P. and Stefanis, C. (1976). Quantitative EEG studies of marihuana, delta-9-THC, and hashish in man. In: *Pharmacology of Marihuana.* Braude, M.C. and Szara, S. (eds.). Raven Press, New York.

19. Ford, R.D. and McMillan, D.E. (1972). Further studies on the behavioral pharmacology of 1-delta-8- and 1-delta-9-THC. Fed. Proc. *31:* 506.

20. Forney, R.B. (1971). Toxicology of marihuana. Pharmacol. Rev. *23:* 279-284.

21. Fried, P.A. (1976). Short- and long-term effects of pre-natal cannabis inhalation upon rat offspring. Psychopharmacologia *50*(3): 285-291.

22. Fried, P. and Charlebois, A. (1976). Cannabis administered during pregnancy; First and second generation effects in rats. (In manuscript.)

23. Gilmour, D.G., Bloom, A.D., Lele, K.P., Robbins, E.S. and Maximilian, C. (1971). Chromosome aberrations in users of psychoactive drugs. Arch. Gen. Psychiatry *24:* 268 1-272.

24. Grinspoon, L. (1969). Marihuana. Sci. Amer. *221:* 17-25.

25. Grinspoon, L. (1971). *Marihuana Reconsidered.* Harvard University Press, Cambridge.

26. Gupta, S., Grieco, M.D. and Cushman, P. (1974). Impairment of rosette-forming T-lymphocytes in chronic marihuana smokers. New Eng. J. Med. *291:* 874-876.

27. Haley, S.L., Wright, P.L., Plank, J.B., Keplinger, M.L., Braude, M.C. and Calandra, J.C. (1973). The effect of natural and synthetic delta-9-tetrahydrocannabinol on fetal development. Toxic. Appl. Pharmacol. *25:* 450 (abstract).

28. Hall, J.A.S. (1974). Testimony before the Senate Subcommittee on Internal Security, May, 1974, ref. 66, pp. 147-154.

29. Harmon, J.W. and Aliapoulios, M.A. (1974). Cited in: Pot smoking and the manly bosom. Medical World News, Dec. 6, 1974.

30. Harper, J.W., Heath, R.G. and Myers, W.A. (1977). Effects of Cannabis sativa on ultrastructure of the synapse in monkey brain. J. Neurosci. Res. *3:* 87-93.

31. Hart, R.H. (1976). A psychiatric classification of cannabis intoxication. J. Amer. Acad. Psychiat. Neurol. *1*(4): 83-97.

32. Heath, R.G. (1972). Marihuana: Effects on deep and surface electroencephalograms of man. Arch. Gen. Psychiat. *26:* 577-584.

33. Heath, R.G. (1973). Marihuana: Effects on deep and surface electroencephalograms of rhesus monkeys. Neuropharm. *12:* 1-14.

34. Heath, R.G. (1974). Testimony before the Senate Subcommittee on Internal Security, May, 1974, ref. 66, pp. 50-70.

35. Heath, R.G. (1974). Data submitted to the Senate Subcommittee on Internal Security, July, 1974, ref. 66, pp. 382-383.

36. Heath, R.G., Fitzjarrell, A.T., Garey, R.E. and Myers, W.A. (1979). Chronic marihuana smoking: Its effects on function and structure of the primate brain, ref. 82a.

37. Hembree, W.C., Zeidenberg, P. and Nahas, G.G. (1976). Marihuana's effects on human gonadal function, ref. 81, pp. 521-532.

38. Hembree, W.C., Huang, H. and Nahas, G.G. (1979). Effects of marihuana smoking on gonadal function of man, ref. 82a.

39. Hollister, L.E., Richards, R.K. and Gillespie, H.K. (1968). Comparison of tetrahydrocannabinol and synhexyl in man. Pharmacol. Ther. 9: 783-791.

40. Hollister, L.E. (1971). Marihuana in man: Three years later. Science 172: 21-24.

41. Huang, H., Hembree, W.C. and Nahas, G.G. (1979). Effects of marihuana smoke on spermatogenesis in rats, ref. 82a.

42. Indian Hemp Drug Commission. (1969). Report on Marihuana of the Indian Hemp Commission, 1893-1894. Thomas Jefferson Press, Silver Springs, Maryland.

43. Isbell, H., Gorodetsky, G.W., Jasinski, D., Claussen, U., Spulak, F. and Korte, F. (1967). Effects of (-) delta-9-tetrahydrocannabinol in man. Psychopharmacologia 14: 115-123.

44. Jacobson, C.B. and Berlin, C.M. (1972). Possible reproductive deficit in LSD users. J. Amer. Med. Assoc. 222: 1367-1371.

45. Jenson, J.N. (1975). Testimony before the Senate Subcommittee on Internal Security, May, 1975, ref. 67, pp. 431-450.

45a. Johnston, L.D., Bachman, J.G. and O'Malley, P.M. (1977). Drug Use Among American High School Students 1975-1977. National Institute on Drug Abuse, Division of Research, Maryland.

46. Jones, H.B. (1974). Testimony before the Senate Subcommittee on Internal Security, May, 1974, ref. 66, pp. 206-250.

47. Jones, H.B. (1976). What the practicing physician should know about marijuana. Private Practice, January, 1976, pp. 34-40.

48. Jones, H.B. and Jones, H.C. (1977). Sensual Drugs: Deprivation and Rehabilitation of the Mind. Cambridge University Press, New York, Cambridge and Sydney.

49. Jones, H.B. (1978). The dangers of cannabis smoking. AMA (Australian Medical Assoc.) Gazette 192: 20-25.

50. Jones, R.T. and Benowitz, N. (1976). The 30-day trip-clinical studies of cannabis tolerance and dependence. In: *Pharmacology of Marihuana,* Braude, M.C. and Szara, S. (eds.). Raven Press, New York, pp. 627-642.

51. Klonoff, H. (1974). Marihuana and driving in real-life situations. Science *186:* 317-324.

52. Knights, R.M. and Grenier, M.L. (1976). Problems in studying the effects of chronic cannabis use on intellectual abilities. In: *Chronic Cannabis Use,* Dornbush, R.L., Freedman, A.M. and Fink, M. (eds.). Ann. N.Y. Acad. Sci. *282:* 307-312.

53. Kolansky, H. and Moore, W.T. (1971). Effects of marihuana on adolescents and young adults. J. Amer. Med. Assoc. *216:* 486-492.

54. Kolansky, H. and Moore, W.T. (1972). Toxic effects of chronic marihuana use. J. Amer. Med. Assoc. *222:* 35-41.

55. Kolodny, R.C. (1974). Testimony before the Senate Subcommittee on Internal Security, May, 1974, ref. 66, pp. 177-126.

56. Kolodny, R.C. (1975). Paper presented at the International Academy of Sex Research meeting, Stony Brook, New York, September, 1975.

57. Kreuz, D.S. and Axelrod, J. (1973). Delta-9-tetrahydrocannabinol: Localization in body fat. Science *179:* 391-393.

58. Kuehnle, J., Mendelson, J.H., Davis, K.R. and New, P.F.J. (1977). Computed tomographic examination of heavy marihuana smokers. J. Amer. Med. Assoc. *237:* 1229-1230.

59. Leuchtenberger, C., Leuchtenberger, R. and Schneider, A. (1973). Effects of marihuana and tobacco smoke on human lung physiology. Nature *241:* 137-139.

60. Leuchtenberger, C. (1974). Testimony before the Senate Subcommittee on Internal Security, May, 1974, ref. 66, pp. 126-142.

61. Leuchtenberger, C., Leuchtenberger, R., Zbinden, J. and Schleh, E. (1976). Cytological and cytochemical effects of whole smoke and of the gas vapor phase from marihuana cigarettes on growth and DNA metabolism of cultured mammalian cells, ref. 81, pp. 243-256.

62. Levy, J.A., Munson, A.E., Harris, L.S. and Dewey, W.L. (1974). Effects of delta-8- and delta-9-tetrahydrocannabinol on the immune response in mice. Pharmacologist *16:* 259.

63. McMillan, D.E., Harris, L.S., Frankenheim, J.M. and Kennedy, J.S. (1970). (1)-delta-9-*trans*-tetrahydrocannabinol in pigeons: Tolerance to the behavioral effects. Science *169:* 501-503.

64. Malcolm, A. (1976). The amotivational syndrome—an appraisal. Addictions *23*(3): 28-49.

65. Manno, J.E. *et al.,* (1976). In: *Marijuana: Effects on Human Behavior,* Miller, L.L. (ed.). Academic Press, New York.

66. *Marihuana-Hashish Epidemic and its Impact on United States Security.* Hearings before the subcommittee to investigate the administration of the Internal Security Act and other internal security laws of the Committee on the Judiciary, United States Senate. (1974). United States Government Printing Office, Washington, D.C.

67. *Marihuana-Hashish Epidemic and its Impact on United States Security: The Continuing Escalation.* Hearings before the subcommittee to investigate the administration of the Internal Security Act and other internal security laws of the Committee on the Judiciary, United States Senate, (1975). United States Government Printing Office, Washington, D.C.

68. Mendelson, J.H., Kuehnle, J., Ellingboe, J. and Babor, T.F. (1974). Plasma testosterone levels before, during and after chronic marihuana smoking. New Eng. J. Med. *291:* 1051-1055.

69. Mendelson, J.H., Babor, T.F., Kuehnle, J.C., Rossi, A.M., Bernstein, J.G., Mello, N.K. and Greenberg, I. (1976). Behavioral and biologic aspects of marijuana use. In: *Chronic Cannabis Use,* Dornbush, R.L., Freedman, A.M. and Fink, M. (eds.). Ann N.Y. Acad. Sci. *282:* 186-210.

70. Miras, C.J. (1969). Experience with chronic hashish smokers. In: *Drugs and Youth,* Wittenborn, J.R., Brill, H., Smith, J.P. and Wittenborn, S.A. (eds.). Charles C Thomas, Springfield, Il, pp. 191-198.

71. Moore, W.T. (1974). Testimony before the Senate Subcommittee on Internal Security, May, 1974, ref. 66, pp. 154-169.

72. Moreau, J. (1845). *Du Hachisch et de L'Alienation Mentale: Etudes Psychologiques.* Libraire de Fortin, Masson, Paris (English edition, Raven Press, New York, 1972).

73. Morishima, A. (1974). Testimony before the Senate Subcommittee on Internal Security, May, 1974, ref. 66, pp. 109-117.

74. Morishima, A., Milstein, M., Henrich, R.T. and Nahas, G.G. (1975). Effects of marihuana smoking, cannabinoids and olivetol on replication of human lymphocytes: Formation of micronuclei. In: *Pharmacology of Marihuana,* Braude, M.C. and Szara, S. (eds.). Raven Press, New York.

75. Morishima, A., Henrich, R.T., Jou, S. and Nahas, G.G. (1976). Errors of chromosome segregation induced by olivetol, a compound with the structure of C-ring common to cannabinoids: Formation of bridges and multipolar divisions, ref. 81, pp. 265-271.

76. Myers, W.A., III and Heath, R.G. (1978). Cannabis sativa: Ultrastructural changes in organelles of neurons in brain septal region of monkeys. J. Neurosci. Res. (In press.)

77. Nahas, G.G. (1973). *Marihuana — Deceptive Weed.* Raven Press, New York.

78. Nahas, G.G., Suciu-Foca, N., Armand, J.P. and Morishima, A. (1974). Inhibition of cell-mediated immunity in marihuana smokers. Science *183:* 419-420.

79. Nahas, G.G. (1974). Testimony before the Senate Subcommittee on Internal Security, May, 1974, ref. 66, pp. 92-108.

80. Nahas, G.G. (1979). *Keep Off the Grass.* Revised edition. Pergamon Press, New York and Oxford.

81. Nahas, G.G., Paton, W.D.M. and Idänpään-Heikkilä, J.E. (eds.). (1976). *Marihuana: Chemistry, Biochemistry and Cellular Effects.* Springer Verlag, New York and Heidelberg.

82. Nahas, G.G., DeSoize, B., Hsu, J. and Miroshima, A. (1979). Effects of delta-9-tetrahydrocannabinol on nucleic acid synthesis and proteins in cultured lymphocytes, ref. 81, pp. 299-312.

82a. Nahas, G.G. and Paton, W.D.M. (eds.) (1979). *Marihuana and Membranes: Quantitation, Metabolism, Cellular Responses, Reproduction and Brain.* Pergamon Press, New York and Oxford. (In press.)

83. Nichols, W.W., Miller, R.C., Heneen, W., Bradt, C., Hollister, L. and Konfer, S. (1974). Cytogenetic studies on human subjects receiving marihuana and delta-9-tetrahydrocannabinol. Mutation Res. *26:* 413-417.

84. Paton, W.D.M. (1974). Testimony before the Senate Subcommittee on Internal Security, May, 1974, ref. 66, pp. 70-79.

85. Penn, I. and Starzl, T.E. (1972). Malignant tumors arising *de novo* in immunosuppressed organ transplant recipients. Transplant. *14:*407-417.

86. Petersen, B.H., Graham, J., Lemberger, L. and Dalton, B. (1974). Studies of the immune response in chronic marihuana smokers. Pharmacologist *16:* 259.

87. Powelson, D.H. (1974). Testimony before the Senate Subcommittee on Internal Security, May, 1974, ref. 66, pp. 18-29.

88. Powelson, D.H. (1974). Marijuana: More dangerous than you know. Reader's Digest (Dec. 1974), pp. 95-99.

89. Rosenkrantz, H. (1976). The immune response and marihuana, ref. 81, pp. 441-456.

90. Rosenkrantz, H. and Braude, M.C. (1976). Comparative chronic toxicities of delta-9-THC administered by inhalation or orally in rats. In: *Pharmacology of Marihuana,* Braude, M.C. and Szara, S. (eds.). Raven Press, New York.

91. Rosenkrantz, H. (1979). Effects of cannabis on fetal development in rodents, ref. 82a.

92. Rosenkrantz, H. and Fleischman, R.W. (1979). Effects of cannabis on lungs, ref. 82a.

93. Rubin, V. and Comitas, L. (1975). *Ganja in Jamaica: A Medical Anthropological Study of Chronic Marihuana Use.* Mouton Press, The Hague.

94. Sassenrath, E.N., Golub, M.S., Goo, G.P. and Chapman, L.F. (1979). Long-term chronic exposure to delta-9-THC: Reproductive deficit and offspring responsiveness in primates, ref. 82a.

95. Sassenrath, E.N., Goo, G.P. and Chapman, L.F. (1979). Behavioral effects of acute and long-term chronic exposure to delta-9-THC in group-living rhesus monkeys, ref. 82a.

96. Schwarz, C.J. (1974). Testimony before the Senate Subcommittee on Internal Security, May, 1974, ref. 66, pp. 200-206.

97. Silverstein, M.J. and Lessin, P.J. (1974). Normal skin test responses in chronic marijuana users. Science *192:* 559-561.

98. Solomon, J., Cocchia, M., Gray, R., Shattuck, D. and Vossner, A. (1976). Uterotrophic effect of delta-9-tetrahydrocannabinol in ovariectomized rats. Science *186:* 740-741.

99. Soueif, M.I. (1974). Testimony before the Senate Subcommittee on Internal Security, May, 1974, ref. 66. pp. 177-182.

100. Soueif, M.I. (1976). Differential association between chronic use and brain function deficits. In: *Chronic Cannabis Use,* Dornbush, R.L., Freedman, A.M. and Fink, M. (eds.). Ann. N.Y. Acad. Sci. *282:* 323-343.

101. Spencer, D.J. (1970). Cannabis induced psychosis. Brit. J. Addict. *65:* 369-372.

102. Stefanis, C.N. and Issidorides, M.R. (1976). Cellular effects of chronic cannabis use in man. ref. 81, pp. 533-550.

103. Stenchever, M.A. and Allen, M.A. (1972). The effect of delta-9-tetrahydro-cannabinol on the chromosomes of human lymphocytes *in vitro*. Am. J. Osbstet. Gynecol. *114:* 819-821.

104. Stenchever, M.A., Kunysz, T.J. and Allen, M.A. (1974). Chromosome breakage in users of marihuana. Am. J. Obstet. Gynecol. *118:* 106-113.

105. Tartaglino, A.C. (1974). Testimony before the Senate Subcommittee on Internal Security, May, 1974, ref. 66, pp. 2-18.

106. Tashkin, D., Calvarese, B. and Simmons, M. (1978). Respiratory status of 74 chronic marijuana smokers: Comparison with matched controls. Paper presented at the annual meeting of the American Lung Association, Boston, Mass., May, 1978.

107. Tennant, F.S., Jr., Preble, M., Prendergast, T.J. and Ventry, P. (1971). Medical manifestations associated with hashish. J. Amer. Med. Assoc. *216:* 1965-1969.

108. Tennant, F.S., Jr. (1974). Testimony before the Senate Subcommittee on Internal Security, May, 1974, ref. 66, pp. 288-314.

109. Waller, C.W. (1975). Testimony before the Senate Subcommittee on Internal Security, May, 1975, ref. 67, pp. 456-460.

110. Weil, A.T. (1972). *The Natural Mind*. Houghton-Mifflin, Boston.

111. Weil, A.T., Zinberg, N.E. and Nelson, J.M. (1968). Clinical and psycho-logical effects of marihuana in man. Science *162:* 1234-1242.

112. West, L.J. (1970). On the marihuana problem. In: *Psychotomimetic Drugs,* Efron, D. (ed.). Raven Press, New York.

113. White, S.C., Brin, S.C. and Janicki, B.W. (1975). Mitogen-induced blasto-genic responses of lymphocytes from marihuana smokers. Science *188:* 71-72.

114. Winkler, F.E. (1970). About marijuana. Myrin Institute, Inc. for Adult Education, New York.

115. Yardley, D.C.M. (1968). Legal aspects of drug dependence in relation to student drug use. In: *The Pharmacological and Epidemiological Aspects of Adolescent Drug Dependents,* Wilson, C.W.M. (ed.). Pergamon Press, Oxford.

116. Zeidenberg, P. (1974). Testimony before the Senate Subcommittee on Internal Security, May, 1974, ref. 66, pp. 189-197.

117. Zimmerman, A.M., Zimmerman, S. and Yesoda Raj, A. (1979). Effects of cannabinoids on spermatogenesis in mice, ref. 82a.

118. Zinberg, N.I. (1976). Untitled article on Marihuana in Psychology Today, Dec. 1976.

Publications Available from The Myrin Institute
521 Park Avenue, New York, New York 10021

Books

	Hard Cover	Soft Cover
The Experience of Knowledge by John F. Gardner	$8.95	$4.50
Man: The Bridge Between Two Worlds by Franz E. Winkler	—	$4.50
For Freedom Destined: Mysteries of Man's Evolution in the Mythology of Wagner's Ring Operas and Parsifal by Franz E. Winkler	$6.95	$3.95
Can the Red Man Help the White Man? ed. by Sylvester M. Morey	—	$1.95
Respect for Life: The Traditional Upbringing of American Indian Children ed. by Sylvester M. Morey and Olivia L. Gilliam	—	$3.50
The Recovery of Man in Childhood by A. C. Harwood	—	$4.95
Laboratory Investigations in Human Physiology by George K. Russell	—	$6.95

Proceedings

*Currently out of print

Proceedings numbers 1 through 31 are sold in bookstores for $1 per copy; Number 32 and subsequent numbers will be sold for $1.50 per copy. Each Proceedings is available directly from the Myrin Institute for a suggested contribution of $1 or more to cover the cost of printing and mailing.

Pamphlets

Contributions Welcomed